P9-EEA-943

DEATH AND REBIRTH IN VIRGIL'S ARCADIA

SUNY Series in Classical Studies
John Peradotto, Editor

DEATH AND REBIRTH IN VIRGIL'S ARCADIA

M. OWEN LEE

State University of New York Press

Published by
State University of New York Press, Albany

Printed in the United States of America

For information, address State University of New York
Press, State University Plaza, Albany, N.Y., 12246

Library of Congress Cataloging-in-Publication Data

Lee, M. Owen, 1930–
    Death and rebirth in Virgil's Arcadia.

    (SUNY series in classical studies)
    Bibliography: p.
    Includes index.
    1. Virgil. Bucolica. 2. Pastoral poetry, Latin—
History and criticism. 3. Death in literature.
4. Regeneration in literature. I. Title. II. Series.
PA6804.B7L44   1989   871'.01   88-24824

ISBN 0-7914-0016-6

ISBN 0-7914-0017-4 (pbk.)

10 9 8 7 6 5 4 3 2 1

In memory of my mother

cantando puerum memini me condere soles

O imaginativa che ne rube
  talvolta sì di fuor, ch'om non s'accorge
  perché dintorno suonin mille tube,

chi move te, se 'l senso non ti porge?
  Moveti lume che nel ciel s'informa,
  per sé o per voler che giù lo scorge.

                              Purgatorio 17.13-8

Contents

Foreword

Günther Jachmann thought the *Eclogues* "the most difficult poems in Latin literature," and William Berg said of them that they "may be the most difficult poetry to survive from the ancient world." Work on them in English, slight by comparison with that devoted to the *Aeneid*, has proceeded apace in the past three decades. My own study has profited greatly from the new insights of an Englishman (Robert Coleman), an Australian (A.J. Boyle), a Canadian (Charles Fantazzi), and several Americans (William Berg, Eleanor Leach, Michael Putnam, and John Van Sickle). Severally and together these Virgilians have helped me, and readers the world over, to see the ten eclogues in ways which now seem new but perhaps were, after all, the ways in which the poet himself saw the poems.

This is not, like theirs, a book for scholars. It is written with some awareness of contemporary scholarship and draws (perhaps too heavily in the case of the land proscriptions) on the ancient lives of and commentaries on Virgil. But it addresses itself first to the reader who wants both an introduction to the *Eclogues* and an interpretation of them.

The interpretation almost demanded of me a personal tone. Arcadia is the land within the imagination where a young poet distances himself from the present and discovers himself. If a man is to find that land, he must travel inwards and, in cases like mine where he is no longer young, backwards in time. I have, accordingly, sometimes spoken in the first person, and introspectively.

As with my book on the *Aeneid*, I have eventually had recourse to the insights, and some of the terminology, of Carl Jung. My final pages are not, however, intended as an explanation of art by way of science. Jung himself proceeded rather in the other direction: "In describing the living process of the psyche, I deliberately give preference to a dramatic, mythological way of thinking and speaking." I have used Jung because Virgil was an intensely intuitive artist, and the psychologies of our century offer us ways of understanding him we ought not to ignore.

For my other extraneous source of reference, Stephen Leacock, I hope I need not apologize. His train to Mariposa really was my means of finding Virgil's Arcadia for the first time, within me (may it bring others there!). And perhaps the lengthy quotation from *Sunshine Sketches* that begins this book is justified by the similarly lengthy quotations that begin other recent studies of the *Eclogues*—quotations from the *Bhagavadgita* and *The French Lieutenant's Woman*.

The text used is the Oxford text of Sir Roger Mynors. Citations from Servius and Servius Danielis are from the edition of Georg Thilo and Hermann Hagen, and those from the Bible are from the King James translation (the new version in the case of the crux at Genesis 3:15). Translations from Appian are from the Loeb Classical Library edition of Horace White. All other translations are my own. The Latin in the footnotes I have left untranslated. Generally speaking, the footnotes are for the Latined.

For readers who would like a full text and translation of the *Eclogues* I heartily recommend the Penguin Classics volume by Guy Lee (unfortunately no relation). For those who would like Theocritus as well I suggest *The Poems of Theocritus* (Chapel Hill, 1978) by Anna Rist (fortunately a good friend).

I must express my thanks to William Eastman of State University of New York Press for his encouragement, to the press's anonymous readers for many helpful remarks, to David Belyea and John O'Connor for reading parts of the manuscript, and to John Grant, chairman of the Department of Classics at the University of Toronto, for providing me with a sabbatical leave which matched Michael Putnam's description of the pastoral, to wit "personal liberty to create in an atmosphere of integrity and order." That means that I should thank above all the truly idyllic cities of London (where I wrote) and New York (where I re-wrote). They provided many books and much art and music, all of which took me inwards, where Arcadia lies.

Acknowledgements

Text of Virgil reprinted by permission of the publishers from the Oxford Classical Text of R. A. B. Mynors, Oxford: Clarendon Press, 1969.

Translation of Appian reprinted by permission of the publishers and the Loeb Classical Library from *Appian's Roman History*, Vol. IV, translated by Horace White, Cambridge, Mass.: Harvard University Press, copyright 1961 by the President and Fellows of Harvard College.

Quotation from *Sunshine Sketches of a Little Town*, by Stephen Leacock, used by permission of the Canadian Publishers, McClelland and Stewart, Toronto.

Quotation from *The Ten Pains of Death*, by Gavin Maxwell, used by permission of Gavin Maxwell Enterprises Ltd., copyright © Gavin Maxwell Enterprises Ltd 1959.

Cover: The "Star Child" from *2001: A Space Odyssey*, © 1968 Metro-Goldwyn-Mayer Inc.

I

Mariposa

Frost's Vermont or Housman's Shropshire or Yeats' Innisfree—any might serve the reader of English as an introduction to what Virgil called Arcadia. My own journey there begins a few blocks from the University of Toronto, where I teach.

It leaves the city every day about five o'clock in the evening, the train for Mariposa.

Strange that you did not know of it, though you come from the little town—or did, long years ago.

Odd that you never knew, in all these years, that the train was there every afternoon, puffing up steam in the city station, and that you might have boarded it any day and gone home. . .

But if you have half forgotten Mariposa, and long since lost the way to it, you are only like the greater part of the men here in this Mausoleum Club in the city. Would you believe it that practically every one of them came from Mariposa once upon a time, and that there isn't one of them that doesn't sometimes dream, in the dull quiet of the long evening here in the club, that some day he will go back. . .

No wonder they don't know about the five o'clock train for Mariposa. Very few people know about it. Hundreds of them know that there is a train that goes out at five o'clock, but they mistake it. Ever so many of them think it's just a suburban train. . .

But wait a little, and you will see that when the city is well behind you, bit by bit the train changes its character. The electric locomotive that took you through the city tunnels is off now and

1

the old wood engine is hitched on in its place. I suppose, very probably, you haven't seen one of these wood engines since you were a boy forty years ago—the old engine with a wide top like a hat on its funnel, and with sparks enough to light up a suit for damages once in every mile.

Do you see, too, that the trim little cars that came out of the city on the electric suburban express are being discarded now at the way stations, one by one, and in their place is the old familiar car with the stuff cushions in red plush (how gorgeous it once seemed!) and with a box stove set up in one end of it? The stove is burning furiously at its sticks this autumn evening, for the air sets in chill as you get clear away from the city and are rising up to the higher ground of the country of the pines and the lakes.

Look from the window as you go. The city is far behind now and right and left of you there are trim farms with elms and maples near them and with tall windmills beside the barns that you can still see in the gathering dusk. There is a dull red light from the windows of the farmstead. It must be comfortable there after the roar and clatter of the city, and only think of the still quiet of it.

As you sit back half dreaming in the car, you keep wondering why it is that you never came up before in all these years. . .

It is almost night now. You can still see the trees and the fences and the farmsteads, but they are fading fast in the twilight. They have lengthened out the train by this time with a string of flat cars and freight cars between where we are sitting and the engine. But at every crossway we can hear the long muffled roar of the whistle, dying to a melancholy wail that echoes in the woods; the woods, I say, for the farms are thinning out and the track plunges here and there into great stretches of bush—tall tamarack and red scrub willow and with a tangled undergrowth of brush that has defied for two generations all attempts to clear it into the form of fields.

Why, look, that great space that seems to open out in the half-dark of the falling evening—why, surely yes, Lake Ossawippi, the big lake, as they used to call it, from which the river runs down to the smaller lake—Lake Wissanotti—where the town of Mariposa has lain waiting for you there for thirty years.

This is Lake Ossawippi surely enough. You would know it anywhere by the broad, still, black water with hardly a ripple, and with the grip of the coming frost already on it. Such a great sheet of blackness it looks as the train thunders along the side, swinging the curve of the embankment at a breakneck speed as it rounds the corner of the lake. . .

Don't tell me that the speed is only twenty-five miles an hour. I don't care what it is, I tell you, and you can prove it for yourself if you will, that that train of mingled flat cars and coaches that goes tearing into the night, its engine whistle shrieking out its warning into the silent woods and echoing over the dull still lake, is the fastest train in the whole world. . .

What? It feels nervous and strange to be coming here again after all these years? It must indeed. No, don't bother to look at the reflection of your face in the window-pane shadowed by the night outside, Nobody could tell you now after all these years. Your face has changed. . .

There—you hear it?—the long whistle of the locomotive, one, two, three! You feel that sharp slackening of the train as it swings round the curve of the last embankment that brings it to the Mariposa station. See, too, as we round the curve, the row of the flashing lights, the bright windows of the depôt.

How vivid and plain it all is. Just as it used to be thirty years ago. There is the string of the hotel buses drawn up all ready for the train, and as the train rounds in and stops hissing and panting at the platform, you can hear above all other sounds the cry of the brakemen and the porters:

"MARIPOSA! MARIPOSA!"

("L'Envoi. The Train to Mariposa,"
. *Sunshine Sketches of a Little Town*)

I quote Stephen Leacock, and at length, in the hope that his imaginary flight back in time to boyhood and lost innocence will provide something of what we first must have to feel our way back into Virgil's pastoral poems today. Too often in the past his "selections", the *Eclogues,* have been thought—to use only once that inevitable but in this context intolerably inappropriate word—artificial. To use such a word is to confuse Virgil's achievement with a later tradition, and a false one—the pastoral that expressed itself in such extravagances as the Petit Trianon, the hoopskirts, minuets and periwigs that vanished with the French revolution. Virgil's pastorals are not so pretty and never, I think, so false. But to see the truth in them the reader must travel, in his imagination, and remember. Strange that he does not know.

I did not know. I spent the summers of my university years working and playing in the very landscape Stephen Leacock calls Mariposa (called Orillia on the map), near its little town in the sunshine, near its black lake (blue-green in the daytime), on the island he calls Indian's (and we called Strawberry). I read Homer, Theocritus, Catullus, and Virgil on that island, sprawled on the grass on a high cliff or propped up against a birch tree or drifting in a boat on the blue-green lake. I wrote songs and sang them there in that Mariposa. I enjoyed the companionship of brothers with the same hopes and dreams as I. And yet, to my shame, I never in my college days related any of that experience to the *Eclogues* of Virgil. It never occurred to me to do so. I wasn't, in the Honour Course in Classics at the University of Toronto (where the Virgil editions of Conington and Page frowned on the *Eclogues*), encouraged to do so. I read Thucydides and Tacitus to learn why men build empires, and Plato and Lucretius to discover what the soul is, and what the world means. Not the *Eclogues*.

Leacock too was educated at the University of Toronto, and before that at Toronto's Upper Canada College. He soon regretted that the years spent learning to read Latin and Greek left him unprepared to face the world, took a second degree in economics and political science, rose quickly in that part of the academic world and, when he took to writing humor and satire, reserved his sharpest barbs for his classical training. "Homer and Humbug" was followed by "What Good Is Latin?" and "My Education and What I Think Of It Now." From the last of these, I can recall one comment on pastoral poetry ("A Greek professor, especially if growing old and apt to sit under a tree and fall asleep over Theocritus, will tell you, of course, that Greek literature is unsurpassed"). But I remember no mention of the *Eclogues*, though they ought to have meant much to Leacock, for he says of his youth, with practiced rue, "That was during the hard times of Canadian farming, and my father was just able by a great diligence

to pay the hired men and, in years of plenty, to raise enough grain
to have seed for the next year's crop without buying any. By this
process my brothers and I were inevitably driven off the land, and
have become professors, business men, and engineers, instead of
being able to grow up as farm labourers."[1]

All the same, though memories of Virgil seem not to have
prompted them consciously, Leacock's *Sunshine Sketches of a
Little Town* often echo the *Eclogues*. His Mariposa is an Arcadia
where Dean Drone reads pastoral poetry to the sound of bees
beneath the plum trees, where ineffectual Peter Pupkin courts shy
Zena Pepperleigh, where Myra Thorpe of the golden hair and
Greek face teases her lovers and astonishes all at poetry readings,
where the enormous Mr. Smith, "with his shepherd's plaid
trousers," has a face that "would make the Mona Lisa seem an
open book and the ordinary human countenance as superficial as a
puddle in the sunlight," though "I don't suppose there were ten
people in Mariposa who knew that Mr. Smith couldn't read."
These figures are not far from Tityrus, Corydon, Phyllis,
Amaryllis, and Silenus. In Virgil.

The Mariposa Belle, a steamer that "goes nowhere in
particular," has "some of those strange properties that distinguish
Mariposa itself. I mean, her size seems to vary so." Mariposa or its
steamer can be "a pathetic little thing the size of a butternut" or,
"after you've *been* in Mariposa for a month or two," as large as the
world itself. Similarly, the Mariposans are, when it suits them, not
Canadian at all, but English or Scottish or Irish or American—
without, of course, ever ceasing to be Canadian. The feeling is as
fluid as in Virgil's pastoral pictures, where nothing is fixed, where
sizes and vistas and identities seem endlessly shifting and elusive.

In Mariposa's barber shop on a sunny afternoon, "what with
the quiet of the hour, and the low drone of Jeff's conversation, the
buzzing of the flies against the window pane, and the measured tick
of the clock above the mirror, your head [sinks] dreaming on your
breast and the place becomes "a very Palace of Slumber." This
memory of the little town "almost within echo of the primeval
forest" is surely Arcadian: Virgil's Tityrus pipes in the shade,
lulled gradually to sleep by the murmuring of innumerable bees in
the willow flowers, by the distant song of the tree-pruner on the
height, by the cooing of the turtle dove from an airy elm.

The surface naiveté, the return to childhood, the intimations of mortality, the elusiveness of outline but clarity of feeling, the sense of a world less complex and troubled than the one we know—all of this in Leacock is Virgilian. It is truer to Virgil's Arcadia than are the porcelain shepherdesses from eighteenth-century salon tables because its author, writing in a large urban center, found it in his imagination, in nostalgic feelings, in vague regrets and, just possibly, in the memory of a harsh reality that invaded a rural life lost beyond recall. The threat of a still harsher reality hung over the readers of Leacock's book at the time it achieved its greatest popularity. The academic who introduces the new printing writes:

> It was the autumn of 1942, in a high-school classroom, when I first heard the whistle of the train to Mariposa . . . I am not sure why it appealed so strongly to us, since we were too fresh from childhood to regard it as long lost . . . Perhaps it was because the Mariposa train seemed like a sort of time machine that took passengers to a period and a place where the murderous violence of 1942 did not exist . . . The real trains that we knew departing from Union Station were carrying friends to the coast en route to European battlefields where some of them had already been mutilated or killed. It was easy to understand why that old fellow in the Mausoleum Club longed to go back to "the little Town in the Sunshine." We would have liked to visit the place, too.[2]

Ever since Virgil, war and death have lurked in the foreground of the pastoral, as the writer recedes in memory to a simpler time.

Finally there is the hint in Leacock that the return to Mariposa is a journey of self-discovery. The little town may be bathed in perennial sunshine, but the train thereto arrives at night, when the traveler's face is reflected in the window pane. He is instructed, as he arrives, not to look at that face. It has changed. His true self will be found in the memory of an earlier time, in morning's sunlight.

Though the traveler may not always realize it, the understanding of himself is, in the end, his reason for making the trip to the place fondly remembered in the past.

There is much too in Virgil that is not in Leacock or Frost or Housman or Yeats. But their landscapes created out of Ontario, New England, England, and Ireland are good places to start from. From Toronto, if you can find your way to the right track at Union

Station, you can travel to Mariposa, even as Virgil traveled in his imagination from Rome[3] to Arcadia. But the first to make this kind of literary journey was Theocritus, who moved in memory from Egyptian Alexandria to the place of his boyhood, Sicily. And to Theocritus we first turn.

II

Sicilia

The pastoral was discovered in the first part of the third century B.C. by a Sicilian poet, Theocritus of Syracuse,[1] when he was living, with many other Greek-speaking litterati of his day, in the new cosmopolitan city of Alexandria, in Egypt.

Alexandria then was a megalopolis, a kind of super-Toronto. It had a brilliant court presided over by Ptolemy Philadelphus and his queen and sister Arisonoë, a lighthouse that was one of the wonders of the world, a library of several hundred thousand volumes, a circle of poet-scholars (more erudite, perhaps, than good poets should be), a vast sprawl of splendors and slums, and an immense and, from descriptions by Theocritus and others, highly excitable polyglot population of some eight hundred thousand people from all parts of the Mediterranean and beyond—for Ptolemy also held lands in Phoenicia, Arabia, Syria, Libya, Ethiopia, and much of Greece.

The description of the celebrations that surrounded Ptolemy's coronation, preserved in Athenaeus,[2] all but defies belief: on the palace roof, a series of awnings embroidered with mythological designs, supported by pillars shaped like palm tees, encircled by arcades draped with the skins of exotic animals; the floor covered with red roses and white lilies, the rooms decked with a hundred statues and paintings and tapestries and a frieze of gold and silver shields; the tables strewn with golden flagons and salvers, the throne room thronged with people masquerading as gods, satyrs, nymphs, bacchants and seasons, clad in purple raiment or wearing golden wings amid the incense that rose from hundreds of swinging censers—and all of this was only part of the ceremonial. Theocritus himself describes, in one of his best poems (*Idyll* XV, the so-called

8

Adoniazusae), the visit made by two gossiping matrons, Sicilian Alexandrians like himself, to a festival in honor of the dying god Adonis: "Lord, what a crowd!" says one of the ladies. "How in the world are we supposed to get through this mess? They're swarming like ants . . . Oh, here come the king's war horses! (My good man, don't trample me down!) Look! The chestnut charger is rearing up! What a wild one he is! (Will you get out of my way, Eunoë? You slaves ought to know your place.) That charger is going to kill his trainer! (It's a good thing I had the sense to leave my brat of a child at home.)"

Most of what we think we know of Theocritus' life in crowded Alexandria is conjecture derived from his poems. (The same is true of what we know of Virgil's life at the time he wrote the *Eclogues*.) Theocritus does not seem to have been thought one of the more important poets in Alexandria's famous library, though he tried his hand at many of the preferred Alexandrian genres. One of these, a popular entertainment raised to literary respectability, was the mime, in which some vivid scene was briefly dramatized. Theocritus' poem about the two women braving the crowd at the festival is a mime, as are his dialogue between two men about mistresses and army life (*Idyll* XIV), his conversation between two fishermen (*Idyll* XXI), and his famous song of a love-mad woman attempting to win her man through magic (*Idyll* II). Theocritus also wrote narrative poems on the myths of Hylas drawn by the nymphs into their watery home (*Idyll* XIII), of Castor victorious with the sword and Polydeuces with the boxing gloves (*Idyll* XXII), of Pentheus dismembered by the women of Thebes (*Idyll* XXVI). He wrote an epithalamium on the wedding of Helen and Menelaus (*Idyll* XVIII), and so many short poems on Heracles we may suppose he planned a larger piece, perhaps even an epic, on the subject (although the Alexandrian writers favored short poems). In addition we have from Theocritus epigrams, love lyrics both hetero- and homosexual, and panegyrics in praise of Ptolemy and other rulers.

But it was yet another genre that secured his immortality. It was something new—a studied withdrawal from bustling Alexandria to remote Sicily and its shepherds, a conjured-up vision of the place where he was born. Like many inventors, Theocritus did not, in the ten short poems that comprised the new genre, set out to create something altogether new, nor did he give his invention the name it has subsequently borne. Pastoral is a modern critical term, used to describe a long tradition often quite different from, and even alien to, the art of its founder.[3] Later pastoral is delicate, where Theocritus is more often rough-and-ready, metaphorical where Theocritus is more often vividly picturesque, essentially serious where Theocritus is more often light-heartedly ironic. And Theocritus would not, in any case, have used a Latin word for shepherd (*pastor*) to characterize his work. As in fact there are more cowherds than shepherds in his pastoral poems, they have come to be called, from the Greek for cowherd, bucolics. In the end, all the poems of Theocritus—mimes, myths, pastorals and the rest—came to be called idylls (*eidyllia*, "little pictures", "sketches" or "vignettes").

The ten poems which shaped the pastoral tradition, numbered I and III–XI in the collection as we have it, were gathered together in a single volume by one Artemidorus,[4] a scholar of Virgil's century, two hundred years after they were written, and it is almost surely that collection that Virgil knew and used—hence his limiting his own pastoral output to ten poems. That is not to say that there are no pastoral touches in the rest of Theocritus. One of the mimes—the love-mad woman's incantation—Virgil was in fact to use for his pastoral purposes. (That might explain why, in the later manuscript tradition, that one mime was set, as number II, near the beginning of the Theocritan corpus, along with the pastorals proper.)

Theocritus' pastorals—or idylls, as we shall henceforth call them—are almost as far removed from crowded, luxurious Alexandria as an emigré Sicilian could imagine them and still keep them within the bounds of Alexandrian taste. They were written mainly to be read by Theocritus' erudite and cantankerous fellow poets in the library. I would venture to say that to some degree they are designed to express critical judgements of those poets. A passage in *Idyll* VII, where the goatherd Lycidas smilingly says "I hate those birds of the Muses that strive in vain with their cackling to match the minstrel of Chios," is an encouragement to read more of the *Idylls* as Theocritus' assessment of the would-be Homers of Alexandria.

Among these were the learned, witty, and authoritative

Callimachus, who shaped his poems into intricate patterns, kept them light (*kata lepton,* "in the slender style," was his motto) and short ("A big book," he said, "is a big bore."); the scholarly Apollonius Rhodius, who rebelled against the master and wrote a big book, an epic on Jason and the Argonauts; the bawdy Herondas, who wrote mimes; and other scholar-poets who wrote the mini-epics we now call *epyllia,* in which two or more myths were intertwined and layered over with learning. I like to think that Callimachus at least was gracious enough to welcome Theocritus' new experiments,[5] even if the others may have thought them outlandish, for between themselves and any dirt-poor and unlettered Sicilian rustics there was, after all, a great gulf fixed. Yet, if we read the poems rightly, here is the genius in them: Theocritus pretends that that gulf is not there, that there was no appreciable difference between the shepherd and the scholar, between the simple and the self-consciously artful man.

So the first pastorals are, to a degree at least, the kind of poems later pastoral became, a species of literary allegory, poems *à clef.* But more than that, the *Idylls* are a projection of the experience of complex city life onto a simple rustic world fondly remembered. From Alexandria Theocritus recalled his boyhood in Sicily (where from his Syracuse it was only a short ride to the shepherds on the hills), and his stay on the island of Cos (where he learned something of his craft among the local literary circles),[6] and he turned his memories of those sunny islands, with their volcanic heights and singing herdsmen, to his own sophisticated purposes, maintaining a delicate balance between sentimental nostalgia and irony, humor and pathos, the realistic and the stylized. Through all of his unurban genre scenes, his main concerns remained the lyricist's concern (love), the poet's concern (music), and the one inevitable fact of life (death). In fact, he began his collection with a Sicilian myth that touched on all three of these—a song of the shepherd dying for love.

The subject matter of the *Idylls* is as follows:

Idyll I: On the slopes of Mt. Etna, a shepherd meets a goatherd and, in the shade of the pine trees, by a stream that drips from a high rock, sings in exchange for a beautifully figured bowl the song of Daphnis: as the wild creatures of nature weep, Daphnis the young Sicilian shepherd hero dies, visited by the three gods Hermes, Priapus, and Aphrodite, bereft of his music and willing his own death as an escape from the torments of love.

(*Idyll* II: In a house by the sea, under a midnight moon, a woman mad with love tries unsuccessfully to make her former lover come back to her, using music, a magic wheel, and voodoo-like rituals.)

Idyll III: In a cavern by the sea, a goatherd who has left his flock in another's care threatens to leap into the waves if his beloved continues to reject him.

Idyll IV: In a glade, two cowherds talk of rustic happenings both happy and sad (the girl in *Idyll* III has died). Then one removes a thorn from the other's foot.

Idyll V: Amid malodorous goatskins, a goatherd and a shepherd quarrel, then engage in a plain-spoken singing contest, judged by a woodcutter. The goatherd wins.

Idyll VI: Beside a well, an older and a younger herdsman, evenly matched in song, tell how once in Sicily the ugly cyclops Polyphemus tried to woo the beautiful sea nymph Galatea. The two herds then kiss and exchange gifts.

Idyll VII: On the island of Cos, Theocritus himself (under the pseudonym Simichidas), accompanied by two friends, meets the goatherd Lycidas who gives him a poet's staff and, with a clear reference to Alexandria, sings of pastoral themes. Theocritus in turn sings about his fellow Alexandrian poets in shepherd's terms, and then proceeds with his two friends to a harvest festival, described in loving detail.

Idyll VIII: In the mountains of Sicily, overlooking the sea, a young shepherd and a young cowherd engage in an exchange of song, and a goatherd judges the young cowherd best.[7]

Idyll IX: The poet bids the same two herdsmen sing again and, when they do so, rewards them both with rustic prizes.

Idyll X: A reaper, inept at his work, sings delicately of the pain of unfulfilled passion. His fellow laborer, good at his work, sings a hearty harvest song.

Idyll XI: The poet, to console a lovesick physician, sings once more of the monster Polyphemus—this time how he first fell in love with Galatea, offered her nature's plenty and then, after his failure to win her, consoled himself in song.

Some further details must be added to this description, as we shall not treat the *Idylls* here in their original Greek. They use a broad Dorian dialect, very likely a studied attempt at reproducing Sicilian speech in terms intelligible to Alexandrian litterati. They are delightful to speak and listen to, highly onomatopoeic. They are composed in the dactylic hexameter, the meter that had served Homeric bards for a thousand years or more. And they very often break the hexameter line after the fourth foot, leaving the music abruptly hanging on two short syllables. This was a pause Homer long before had used, often to change a scene or score a rhetorical point. Theocritus used this Homeric pause, or diaeresis, so extensively that it has come to be called, even in Homeric studies, the bucolic (i.e., pastoral) diaeresis.

Literary critics in antiquity classified the pastoral as a subspecies of epic, and it is possible that from the start Theocritus thought of his *Idylls* as a scaling down of epic Homer into "little pictures," with Homer's characters ironically and even comically recast.[8] The shepherd world is not as far as we might think from the world of Homer's heroes. Similes in the *Iliad* sometimes introduce into their comparisons from nature a shepherd gladding in his heart or a goatherd shuddering at an advancing stormcloud. On the warlike shield of Achilles in *Iliad* XVIII we find depictions of shepherds happy at their piping, then slaughtered in an ambush (520–6), cowherds and their dogs rushing to the rescue of a bull attacked by lions (573–86), and a boy at harvest time playing the lyre and singing a song of the death of the shepherd-god Linus—a song, that is to say, about the end of summer (569–71). When, in

Iliad XXII, Hector nerves himself to face Achilles, a little song stays in his head, seemingly irrelevant but psychologically right, for he is repressing the thought of his wife; the song, "from oak or rock like lad and lass," may preserve the myth of the origins of humans from rocks after the deluge and from oaks in the land where Virgil was to set his pastoral, Arcadia. These small harbingers of pastoral are not mere descriptive set pieces; taken together, they make the essential Iliadic point that war is not, nor should it be, the norm in human life.

Even stronger are the anticipations of pastoral in Homer's *Odyssey*, with its formulaic passage about happily-ever-aftering gods; with its lovingly detailed descriptions of remote, idyllic islands; with its hero welcomed home by his faithful swineherd, helped by his cowherd, betrayed by his goatherd; and above all with the figure of the cyclops Polyphemus, a monstrous shepherd but a shepherd nonetheless, grieving as he strokes the fleece of his great ram while unbeknownst to him the plucky hero hangs beneath clutching the ram's fleece and ready to escape. When, centuries later, Theocritus turned Homer's frightening but easily fooled monster to an amorous suitor both comic and pathetic, he affirmed the pastoral's everlasting debt to epic: the new genre is one that selects a few details in Homer and finds in them new potential. Who would have thought Polyphemus could have a whole new lease on literary life? Perhaps only another Sicilian would have; Theocritus calls the monster *redivivus* "my compatriot."

Theocritus may also have drawn some of his first ideas for the pastoral from Hesiod, who represented himself as inspired by the Muses as he tended flocks. He certainly drew on the sometime Sicilian poet Stesichorus who, in a choral ode we know of only at second hand, told the myths of the Sicilian shepherd Daphnis. We cannot reconstruct Daphnis' cycle of myths (Theocritus and Virgil write mainly of his death), but Stesichorus made him the son of the god Hermes, tending no ordinary flock but the sacred oxen of the Sun; his death may then once have symbolized the end of the solar year.

Still more authors contributed to the shaping of the pastoral. The famous descriptions of nature as a place of innocence (73–87) or escape (743–51) in Euripides' *Hippolytus,* or as a place that, in Plato's *Phaedrus* (229A–230E), seduces the thinker from his thought, may well have influenced the poet of nature put down in crowded Alexandria. Certainly Theocritus drew on Epicurus, whose doctrines were widely preached and practiced in the Alexandrian world, who anticipated the pastoral impulse when he withdrew from his city, Athens, to cultivate inner peace and the quiet joys of friendship in his garden.

It should not be thought, however, that Theocritus' pastoral world is derived only from literary sources. Practical details in his *Idylls* are acutely observed, seemingly at first hand. And in fact some of the same details may still be observed among herdsmen in Sicily twenty-three centuries later, as witness this extraordinary contemporary record provided by a fifteen-year-old Sicilian cowherd, transcribed by Gavin Maxwell:

> I'm a cowherd at Don Paolo's, my employer—he's rich and he's got a lot of cows. I have to stay with the cows in the mountains from the morning till the evening, taking them to graze and milking them in the evening, and do you know how much Don Paolo gives me a week? 1,050 lire. He says that's 250 lire a day. . .
>
> While the animals graze I pass the time playing my flute and singing, lying in the shade of a rock or tree. All the herd boys like me have flutes—we make them ourselves out of thick bamboo stems and when we make a good one we keep it for ever. I can do bird-songs on my flute, too, and you can have a wonderful time doing that, getting the birds to answer you one after another. I play herd songs a lot of the time, and when I meet another herdboy we play part songs. I can sing hundreds of verses of songs—I love them—and I've learnt dozens and dozens from other herdboys I've met in the mountains. The songs go on for ever, and there's as many verses as grains of sand on the seashore. One learns more every day and makes up more every day—I could sing right through the night until dawn without repeating a verse twice . . . This one starts off all right:
>
> > Turn to me my lovely one and hear me sing
> > For my voice will touch your heart. . .
>
> > Do not leave me
> > Or I shall kill myself

You know that for you
I am driven to madness.

But then the lover gets angry at being left, and after a bit he's
singing very dirty words.

"Beyond this point," says Maxwell, "the verses are unprintable in
English; I have left them in Sicilian in the appendix." The young
Sicilian continues:

Then there's songs you sing in alternate verse with someone you
can hear but most times can't see. These are called *botta e
riposta*. We herds don't often meet each other in the mountains—
each of us takes his animals to different places because there's not
enough grass to go round, but we can play games together even if
we're far apart. You hear the voice of another herd singing far
away and you wait for the right moment and answer him. If he
hears you start up alternate verses like this:

I sing: Who are you that's singing up there?
          You sound like a yapping puppy.
and he answers: And who are you wailing away down there?
          You sound as if you had a toothache in every tooth.
I: You know nothing about singing—
          You'd better go and learn at school in Palermo.
He: You say I don't know how to sing—
          You'd better go to school at Monreale.
I: Don't you come round here again—
          Everyone says you're a cretin.
He: It's you that's got to quit this valley—
          Everyone knows about you.
I: When you were born behind my door
          I thought you were a still-born bitch pup.
He: When you were born in the middle of my street
          There was an awful stink of dung.

The Sicilian boy sang twenty-seven such verses, till they climaxed,
according to Maxwell, "in a perfect orgy of sexual abuse and
sexual boasting." The boy then observed:

But that would be far too short for a real *botta e riposta*; I've left out a hundred verses in the middle. If one of us stopped as soon as that the other would think he'd had an accident. Sometimes I've sung a *botta* for the whole night—one's voice sounds better at night. We don't take offense at what we sing to each other—if we did we wouldn't sing them, or else we'd go and beat each other up. If you're clever enough you can invent new verses, but you have to make them rhyme properly.[9]

Much of Theocritus is very close to this—love-sick songs that end in death, or exchanges (the technical name is amoebean verses) in which the second singer re-arranges the words of the first to get the better of him. Theocritus tuned his songs, of course, to the taste of his citified Alexandrian listeners, and left it to his fellow poets in the library to say whether the *botte e riposte* he'd recreated had any reference, *mutatis mutandis,* to their own disputes about poetry and pride-of-place.

The new genre, however skillfully conceived and realized, was limited in scope, and the lively Sicilian among the effete scholar poets would likely have been the first to admit as much. He would also doubtless have been astonished, if pleased, to hear that his distinctly minor invention had survived and flourished through five centuries in antiquity and then, after slumbering for a thousand years, woke for five centuries more—through Petrarch and Sannazaro to Spenser and Milton to Shelley and Arnold to Housman and Frost. I rather think that it would not have lived so long had it not been for Virgil's contribution, but already in Theocritus there are indications that the pastoral could be much more than a poet's masquerade, more than so many "little pictures" of a remembered past that threw a very different present into relief. Already in Theocritus we find features that mark Virgil's *Eclogues.*

There is, first of all, a sense of nature as a continuum. From rocks and rivers to flowers and trees to birds and beasts to humans and, eventually, gods, all of Theocritus's world feels the same sorrows and joys, all things partake in the one nature that animates them according to their receptiveness. The gods—this is remarkable in poetry ultimately derived from epic—are hardly more important than the fauna and flora that adorn their festivals. Nature is one. The only gods that matter are those who bring fertility (Demeter and Priapus), those who make music (Apollo and his

Muses, Pan and his attendants), and those who make men fall in love (Aphrodite and Eros).

The continuum is made palpable in music, which affects all of nature at the deepest level. Equally pervasive is love—casual, promiscuous, and potentially destructive. (Much of the negative feeling about passionate love comes, of course, from Epicurus.) There is also in Theocritus a suggestion of the pastoral's famous enclosure, the *locus amoenus*,[10] the "pleasance" in which nature, for as long as she can, provides an ideal existence. In *Idyll* VII, the *Thalysia* or "Harvest Festival", the one character in Theocritus we can identify as the poet himself describes the enclosure:

> We laid ourselves happily down on cushiony beds
> Of scented lentisk and new-stripped leaves of vine,
> While high overhead a forest of poplars and elms was waving,
> And close by a sacred stream splashed and sang out from the cave
>   of the nymphs.
> On the shaded branches, sun-burnt cicadas kept busy chattering
>   away,
> And the tree-toad was croaking far off in the thick thorn brake.
> Linnets and larks were singing, and the voice of the turtle was
>   heard.
> Yellow bees were zooming here and there around the fountains.
> Everything breathed the scent of rich harvesting and bourgeon-
>   ing.
> Pears were rolling in plenty at our feet, and apples at our sides,
> And branches burdened with plums bowed down to earth.

But, as *Idyll* I is there at the start of the collection to remind us, in the midst of such plenty the archetypal shepherd-poet, Daphnis, dies. He dies although all the rest of life in the continuum wants to save him. He dies to escape the torments of sexual desire, which have taken his song from him. He dies virtually willing his own death. And he dies heroically, proclaiming his victory in the face of his enemy Aphrodite and, like Prometheus or Job, greater in his sufferings than the three who come to question him. Already in Theocritus we find the idea essential to the pastoral myth—that the experience of the pastoral, the intensity of its pleasures, cannot last for long, that death is present too in the shepherd's land. A

conspicuous monument on the landscape of *Idyll* VII, on the way to
the plenteous enclosure, is a tomb:

> We were not yet half-way on our journey,
> And the tomb of Brasilas had not yet come in view. . .

We have to look far into the *Idylls* of Theocritus to find any
traces of a motif that, after Virgil, became very much a part of the
tradition—the end of war and the rediscovery of lost innocence in
the return of a Golden Age. The notion of a long-lost age of
happiness, when men were ever-young, nourished by an
ever-benevolent nature, was as old as Hesiod (*Works and Days*
112–9). But the hope for its return was not expressed in literature
until the Virgilian pastoral took it up. There are, however, some
anticipations of this in Theocritus, in the non-pastoral pieces, and it
is tempting to think that Virgil may have got the idea for his famous
"Messianic Eclogue" from them. One of the passages comes in a
homoerotic context in *Idyll* XII:

> Would it were, O father Zeus and all you ageless gods,
> That it might come to pass,
> That two hundred generations hence someone might come to me
> At Acheron's uncrossable stream, and say,
> "Ah, surely then there were golden men on earth,
> When friends gave love for love."

The other comes in *Idyll* XVI, a song in praise of Hiero, the
champion of Sicily after its devastation by the Carthaginians:

> May there come a time when our cities, despoiled by enemy
>   hands,
> Are filled again with their people of old.
> May our folk till the fruitful fields.
> May sheep by the thousands, past numbering, fatten on the grass
>   and bleat along the plain . . .
> May spiders spin their delicate web upon the weapons of war,
> May the cry of battle never more be named.

Finally in Theocritus we find, perhaps more beautifully stated
than in Virgil, the conferring of his mission on the poet. Once

again, this comes in the all-important *Idyll* VII. There the mysterious, smiling goatherd named Lycidas meets the Simichidas ("snub-nose") we identify with Theocritus himself and, after an exchange of song, gives him a staff of wild olive as a pledge of brotherhood in the Muses. Virgil will remember this symbolic bestowal of an older poetic tradition on a younger man equipped to continue it. He will also use Lycidas in one of his finest poems.

So Theocritus gave Virgil something of what he needed for his first major work — the projection of a complex, crowded present onto a simpler, fondly remembered past; shepherd figures like Lycidas and Daphnis who speak for poets; a natural world that responds to the shepherds' music and suggests moderation in their love-making; an enclosure where trouble is, at least for the moment, unknown; the suggestion that, though death is an ever-present reality, the lost innocence mankind still remembered might someday return; and the sense of a tradition passed on.

Virgil's poems came to be called eclogues, "selections" — a strange name, and one never quite completely explained. But when this reader comes to Virgil fresh from Theocritus he finds it hard to dismiss that thought that the poems were called eclogues because in them Virgil "selects" poetic ideas from his deft Alexandrian predecessor to use for his own even more sophisticated ends.

III

Mantua

Virgil was born in 70 B.C., in the district called Andes, near Mantua, in the province of cis-Alpine Gaul. He was probably of Celtic stock.[1] The river Mincius irrigated the land, which was Po-valley rich, and the young Virgil lived with his parents (and, possibly, two bothers) a rural life on his father's farm.[2] Rural but congenial. The four books of the *Georgics,* written just after the *Eclogues,* bear this out. They are a fairly realistic description of an agricultural existence, ostensibly didactic, a kind of farmer's manual but also, with gathering force, a poet's revelation of the transfiguring spiritual power that permeates the earth. Virgil loved the land, and he learned to love it early in life.

Through his teens, Virgil was educated at nearby Cremona and then, as he showed promise and the resources of the farm permitted it, in Mantua and—briefly, for politics was not where his future lay—in Rome. Finally in his early twenties he found, in the Naples area, the education that most suited him—in "the Garden" a circle of Epicurean poet-philosophers presided over by an inspiring teacher named Siro. There the literary influence was clearly from Alexandria. Even if we regard as spurious the Alexandrian experiments that have come down to us under Virgil's name—the *Catalepton* and other apparently youthful efforts—the *Eclogues* alone are enough to proclaim the young Virgil a Latin descendent of Callimachus and Theocritus, an Alexandrian miniaturist crafting small, subtle, elegantly finished work. The *Georgics,* written in the Alexandrian didactic tradition and ending with a myth-within-a-myth epyllion, would confirm this. (Stoicism, Homer, and the other traditions that shaped the vast *Aeneid* lay far in the future.)

Why should the literature of Alexandria appeal to a young man from the Po valley? How, for that matter, did Alexandrianism establish itself in Italy, which had long since developed a literature of its own? The main influences are two. An anthology of poems by Alexandrian writers, the *Garland* of Meleager, was widely circulated in Italy a quarter-century before Virgil's birth. And at about the time he was born there came to Italy a poet-teacher, Parthenius of Nicaea, intent on preaching Alexandrian poetics. Soon there was a generation of enthusiastic young Roman Callimachans—Catullus, Cinna, Calvus, Caecilius—ready to rebel against the older, and to them outdated, Italian traditions. Alexandria was their lodestar. What was studied and effete two centuries before in Alexandria became, in the hands of these talented young men, fresh and creative in Rome.

Cicero called the new rebels, contemptuously, the neoterics; in Latin they were the *poetae novi*. Of their number only Catullus has survived to any degree, and his work is by any standard brilliant. We can sense something of what it was to be alive and in love in Republican Rome from Catullus' shorter poems, which throb with scarcely controlled passion and excitement. We can also sense something of what Alexandrian Callimachus may have been like in the longer, more ambitious poems of Catullus, which are mythical, erudite, and elegantly crafted.

Catullus died at thirty, a little younger than some lyric artists (Propertius, Tibullus, Schubert, Burns), a little older than some others (Shelley, Keats, Rupert Brooke and Wilfred Owen). Virgil began his literary career writing as if he were completing Catullus' work: he wrote in the two Alexandrian modes, pastoral and didactic verse, that Catullus and his friends had left untouched. With the *Eclogues* and the *Georgics* Virgil probably hoped to be, in his quiet way, a successor to the *poetae novi,* a writer in the Roman Alexandrian tradition.

The civil wars were being fought as Virgil began to write. They had waged through most of the century and were not to end until almost a decade after the *Eclogues* were published. They constantly threaten Virgil's pastoral scenes. As he wrote, the land lay unworked or wasted. Blood was split in city and country alike. The sensitive young man from the country, peaceful by nature, came close to despair at times. Both *Eclogues* and *Georgics* are witness to this.

At some point in his twenties (again we have only a few scattered biographical facts), Virgil came in contact with the four political figures who would shape his early life and art—Pollio, Varus, Gallus, and Octavian (soon to become Caesar Augustus). As all of these men figure in the *Eclogues,* some facts about them must be set forth here.

GAIUS ASINIUS POLLIO was an aristocratic man of letters drawn, by disposition perhaps, and from a sense of family honor, into politics. In his teens he had known the gifted Catullus,[3] ten years his senior, and later he wrote poetry of his own, as well as tragedy, rhetoric, literary criticism that was fearless and widely quoted, and above all a history of his own times that was still read a century after his death. All of this, though remarked on by extant authors, is now lost to us. In his political life Pollio supported Julius Caesar, held a command in Spain the year before Caesar's assassination, then lent his support to the man he thought Caesar's legitimate heir, Mark Antony. He was consul in 40 B.C. and, from the riches he won in a triumph over the Illyrians, built the first public library in Rome—after which he retired to his books.

Virgil may have met Pollio first when, in his mid-twenties, he left the school in Naples to return to the family farm. Pollio was then, as lieutenant of Mark Antony and governor of cis-Alpine Gaul, residing in the region around Mantua. He had surrounded himself with a circle of literate friends, and it was he who first suggested to Virgil that he write pastoral poetry[4] and thus prove himself in an Alexandrian genre still unattempted in Latin. Graceful references to Pollio mark the third *Eclogue,* which may be the first in order of composition.

PUBLIUS ALFENUS VARUS was, like Virgil, from the Po valley and of Celtic origins. And like Pollio he had known the poet Catullus.[5] His ambition and intelligence took him to the consulship in 39 B.C. He was the first Transpadane to reach that office. In addition to his political and military life, he published forty volumes of legal treatises still quoted five centuries later. Virgil knew him, if not before, when he succeeded Pollio as governor of cis-Alpine Gaul in 42 B.C. Though Varus was a native son, his policies, as we shall see, did not by any means favor the natives of the region. Virgil's references to him are ambivalent, or at least difficult to interpret.

GAIUS CORNELIUS GALLUS, perhaps the most important of the four for our understanding of the *Eclogues,* and certainly the most tragic, was along with Virgil a protégé of Pollio, and doubtless they saw each other at Pollio's circle. Gallus may in fact have been the finest lyric poet of his day.[6] But of his poetry— some epyllia, or mini-epics, and four books of *Amores* addressed to his mistress under the pseudonym Lycoris—only a few lines survive.[7] He committed suicide at the age of forty-three.

Gallus was, as his cognomen indicates, of Gallic descent, born on the Mediterranean in Forum Julii (modern Fréjus). His poetic tenets were, again, Alexandrian: his epyllia harked back to Theocritus' fellow poets in the library, and his love poems to Lycoris continued the tradition of Catullus' famous lyrics to Lesbia. It is easy to see the handsome, brilliant Gallus dominating discussions at Pollio's circle, debating matters Alexandrian, announcing his intention to write in Latin epyllia all the fascinating, psychologizing myths beloved of the Alexandrian catalogue-poets. It is easy too to see Virgil overawed by the brilliance.

But like our other Romans Pollio and Varus, Gallus the man of letters was also a soldier and politician. He had a brilliant but tragically brief career. He defeated Antony in Egypt, aided in the capture of Cleopatra, served as Octavian's viceroy in the newly-created province of Egypt where he designed a Roman forum (the record of which he inscribed on the obelisk that now stands in front of St. Peter's in Rome), crushed local rebellions (the record of which was statue after statue of himself), and established a Roman buffer state in Ethiopia (the record of which he inscribed on the pyramids). Meanwhile, Octavian, now the first citizen of what was no longer a Roman republic but a Roman empire, had accepted the title Augustus. For reasons we do not know but can perhaps easily divine, he recalled Gallus, formally renounced his friendship with him, prosecuted him and, perhaps, had his writings destroyed. Galls died, not just of his own hand, but in disgrace, his suicide mandated by senatorial decree. This was ten years after Virgil wrote of him in the *Eclogues,* but as we shall see something of it is strangely forecast in the young Virgil's verses.

GAIUS OCTAVIUS, called OCTAVIAN and eventually

CAESAR AUGUSTUS, is fourth and far the greatest of our figures. When the will of Julius Caesar was opened, Octavian was revealed as the adopted son and chief heir of the assassinated leader. Still in his teens, he took it on himself to avenge his adoptive father, challenging first Mark Antony, who had opposed him in the matter of the will, and defeating him at Mutina. He was made consul when his legionaries forced the appointment, and then, to implement the dead Caesar's policies, he joined forces with Antony and Lepidus in what history has called the second triumvirate.

The triumvirs resorted to measures Julius Caesar would not have countenanced. They initiated the series of infamous but, by the special jurisdiction conferred on them, legal proscriptions whereby suspected Roman citizens—Cicero among them—were declared outlaws, their goods confiscated, their lives forfeit. Octavian was at first reluctant to embark on the proscriptions, notorious for their use earlier in the century by Sulla, but once the decision was made he was even more relentless and ruthless than were his fellow triumvirs. So relatives and slaves of the proscribed were encouraged by rewards or coerced by threat of punishment to inform on Roman citizens, and the innocent and the guilty—some three hundred senators and two thousand knights—were hunted down and killed by squads of soldiers throughout Italy. Eventually the triumvirs defeated the assassins of Julius Caesar, Brutus and Cassius, at Philippi in northern Greece. During much of the campaign, Octavian was ill. In fact a rumor reached Rome that, on his return journey, he had died. His recovery was slow but his re-appearance was effective: with his adoptive father Julius now officially proclaimed a god, he could and did style himself *divi filius,* the son of a god. (Virgil was eventually to draw on this "death, rebirth and apotheosis.")

The rest of the remarkable career of Octavian, surely one of the most important figures in the history of mankind, we need not tell here, save for one series of events—those with which the *Eclogues* begin.

After the two battles of Philippi in 42 B.C., the triumvirs agreed that Antony should pacify the East and Octavian lead the veterans, some two hundred thousand of them, back to Italy and pension them off on the land that they had been promised—land which was already or had yet to be confiscated from its owners. It was an unenviable assignment, likely as in the past to lead to more violence and, as was eventually the case, to war. Of course Antony knew of the possibility of this happening and probably saw the assignment as a convenient way of eliminating the ambitious young Octavian.

Land was the most important factor in Italian economy, "the safest investment, and the chief basis of wealth."[8] The overwhelming majority of adult male citizens in Italy in Virgil's day lived on the land. Octavian was faced with having to evict thousands of these. At this point we might let the historian Appian tell the story:

> The task of assigning the soldiers to their colonies and dividing the land was one of exceeding difficulty, for the soldiers demanded the cities which had been selected for them before the war as prizes for their valour, and the cities demanded that the whole of Italy should share the burden, or that the cities should cast lots with the other cities, and that those who gave the land should be paid the value of it; and there was no money. They came to Rome in crowds, young and old, women and children, to the forum and the temples, uttering lamentations, saying that they had done no wrong for which they, Italians, should be driven from their fields and their hearthstones, like people conquered in war. The Romans mourned and wept with them, especially when they reflected that the war had been waged, and the rewards of victory given, not in behalf of the commonwealth, but against themselves and for a change in the form of government; that the colonies were established to the end that democracy should never again lift its head—colonies composed of hirelings settled there by the rulers to be in readiness for whatever purpose they might be wanted.

> Octavian explained to the cities the necessity of the case, but he knew that it would not satisfy them; and it did not. The soldiers encroached upon their neighbors in an insolent manner, seizing more than had been given to them and choosing the best lands; nor did they cease even when Octavian rebuked them and made them numerous other presents, since they were contemptuous of their rulers in the knowledge that they needed them to confirm their power, for the five years' term of the triumvirate was passing away, and army and rulers needed the services of each other for mutual security. . . .

Octavian knew that the citizens were suffering injustice, but he was without means to prevent it, for there was no money to pay the value of the land to the cultivators, nor could the rewards to the soldiers be postponed, on account of the enemies who were still on foot.

(Appian, *Civil Wars* 5.2.12–3, 15)

Appian then records how Octavian's life was threatened by a group of soldiers who thought that he had imprisoned or even executed one of their comrades following an incident in the theater. And later, when Octavian seemed not to be proceeding quickly enough in the land assignments, the soldiers grew mutinous:

Nonius, a centurion, chided them with considerable freedom, urging decent treatment of the commander by the commanded, and saying that the cause of the delay was Octavian's illness, not any disregard of them. They first jeered at Nonius as a sycophant; then, as the excitement waxed hot on both sides, they reviled him, threw stones at him, and pursued him when he fled. Finally he plunged into the river and they pulled him out and killed him and threw his body into the road where Octavian was about to pass along. So the friends of Octavian advised him not to go among them, but to keep out of the way of their mad career. But he went forward, thinking that their madness would be augmented if he did not come. When he saw the body of Nonius he turned aside. Then, assuming that the crime had been committed by a few, he chided them and advised them to exercise forbearance toward each other hereafter, and proceeded to divide the land. He allowed the meritorious ones to ask for rewards, and he gave to some who were not meritorious, contrary to their expectation. Finally the crowd were confounded; they repented and were ashamed of their importunity; they condemned themselves and asked him to search out and punish the slayers of Nonius. He replied that he knew them and would punish them only with their own guilty consciences and the condemnation of their comrades.

(Appian 5.2.16)

But conditions in Rome worsened when famine struck, and the soldiers robbed and killed and went unpunished. Meanwhile, lands were being re-assigned in various parts of Italy. Among the partially dispossessed were the young poets Horace, Tibullus, and

Propertius.[9] Cassius Dio (*Roman History* 49.8) writes, "Many homes were burned down . . . in all the cities alike, wherever the two parties fell in with each other."

Octavian's confiscations were opposed, not just by the landowners, but by the jealous partisans of his fellow triumvirs— especially by Antony's wife Fulvia and his brother Lucius Antonius. They and their armies occupied Rome. Octavian acted immediately with force, and the Antonians took refuge in the old Etruscan hill town of Perusia. Octavian drew elaborate siege-lines around it and kept up the attack for months. The Antonians attempted a series of sorties, but finally surrendered. If we can believe the anti-Augustan sources, there followed an infamous mass execution of three hundred Roman senators and knights, sacrificed on the Ides of March at an altar dedicated to the memory of Julius Caesar. Fulvia escaped to Greece and Lucius Antonius was, perhaps for diplomatic reasons, spared. Perusia, apart from two of its temples, was burned to the ground.

The terror of the event has been caught in a remarkably vivid poem (1.21) by Virgil's slightly younger contemporary Propertius:

> You, hurrying past to escape from the fate that fell to me,
> You, soldier wounded and hurrying past the Etruscan siege-
>   works,
> Why do you twist your straining eyes round as I groan here?
> I was one of your unit. I fought at your side.
> Save yourself! Make your parents happy.
> Let your sister know, from your tears, what has happened:
> I, Gallus, got safely through the midst of Caesar's swords,
> But could not flee from unknown hands.
> And let her know that, of all the bones she finds scattered on
>   these Etruscan hills,
> These bones, on this spot, are mine.

The Gallus here is of course not the poet-statesman who became Virgil's friend, but some soldier of the Antonian forces who fell after the siege of Perusia, either in the mass executions following or, ironically, in some unforeseen mishap during his escape. He addresses, at the moment of death, another fugitive who, ironically again, is the brother of the woman he loves.

Gallus the poet was at the time assigned the duty of collecting taxes from exempted properties in the north. Here is where Virgil's life intersects with the four others, and our reconstruction of the events becomes, for lack of complete evidence, increasingly tentative.[10] Virgil's Mantua was exempted, but his family farm lay not far from a city designated for property seizure, Cremona. For that reason perhaps, he left the school of Siro in Naples and returned to Mantua. As his writings had attracted the attention of Pollio and his circle, the family farm, however extensive it may have been, was probably in no danger so long as Pollio remained governor. But in 42 Pollio resigned; he doubtless had little stomach for Octavian's confiscations, and was in any case a friend of Antony's and so increasingly alienated from Octavian.

Pollio was succeeded by Varus, whom Octavian may have chosen because he was a native Transpadane and eminently fair. (It might be said here that the confiscations were almost the only way Romans had of settling their armies; that most of the veterans were themselves former farmers who wanted peacefully to farm;[11] that the land, neglected or laid waste through almost a century of civil war, desperately needed working; that Octavian himself, once he effected a lasting peace, initiated the necessary reforms in the military and actively promoted the reworking of the countryside.)

Varus did his detestable duty, and what Virgil feared eventually happened: the lands around Cremona were not enough, and the confiscations extended towards his own Mantua. It is likely (from *Eclogue* 9) that the twenty-eight-year-old poet, as the most articulate spokesman for his hapless neighbors, appealed to Varus as a man of letters and Transpadane like himself, promising that, if Mantua were spared, he would write him a poem to further his career: the swans of song (Mantua was known for its singing swans) would bear Varus' name to the skies. Varus may well have been sympathetic, and may have provided a letter of introduction to Octavian, but Virgil was (if we read *Eclogue* 9.11–8 correctly) unsuccessful in his mission, and he and his traveling companion were lucky to have got through the rioting soldiers and the dispossessed with their lives.

We may then suppose (from *Eclogue* 1) that Virgil's farm was confiscated and that he appealed at the highest level in Rome. We know that, in the year 41 B.C., Gallus was criticizing Varus' policies there, in the presence of Octavian. The main charge was that Varus did not allow Mantua sufficient land to live on: he had been authorized to leave a three-mile strip in every direction from the city, and had scarcely allowed the eight hundred paces, mostly water, that lay around it. (Virgil's farm lay just inside the thee-mile strip and ought to have been exempted.) Octavian, at what was perhaps his first encounter with the poet who would later write his epic, granted the reprieve for Virgil and his fellows in the three-mile zone. Nothing, unfortunately, could be done for the other farms farther from Mantua.

Virgil then paid poetic tribute—a decidedly ambivalent tribute—to Octavian in *Eclogue* 1, where an exempted farmer engages in dialogue with one of the dispossessed. Varus never got his "swan's praises": they are elegantly withheld in the poem dedicated to him, *Eclogue* 6. It is Gallus who is singled out in that poem, in a remarkable and unexpected passage in which he is chosen by the Muses as the poetic hope for the future.

The *Eclogues,* it will readily appear from what has been said, were not written in the order in which they were finally published. (The final ordering eventually will be shown to be essential for understanding them as a whole.) Virgil probably wrote *Eclogues* 2 and 3, Theocritus excerpted and Latinized, at the encouragement of Pollio when that friend of poets was still governor in 42 B.C. and was encouraging Virgil to become the Latin Theocritus. *Eclogue* 5, in which 2 and 3 are spoken of as already published, must come later, but only slightly so, as its main concern is the deification of Julius Caesar, also in 42 B.C. *Eclogues* 8 and 7, fairly clearly designed as more sophisticated companion pieces to 2 and 3, probably followed soon thereafter. (The five poems may be thought of as a kind of "Pollio cycle".) Then, after the siege of Perusia, the departure of Pollio from cis-Alpine Gaul, and the evictions under Varus, we can assign to the year 41 B.C. or shortly thereafter *Eclogue* 9 (Virgil's initial, unsuccessful appeal to Varus on behalf of the Mantuans), *Eclogue* 1 (his partially successful appeal to Octavian), and *Eclogue* 6 (his ambivalent feelings about Varus and his continuing fascination with Gallus).

In the autumn of 40 B.C., the troubled political events seemed suddenly to Virgil and the world to be reversed, when Pollio as consul effected a treaty, the Peace of Brundisium, between Antony and Octavian. For the occasion, Virgil drew on several prophetic traditions and wrote the most famous of his short poems, the hopeful "Messianic" *Eclogue* 4. But the peace was short-lived. Pollio resigned and withdrew to Macedonia. Antony and Octavian, with power in separate parts of the world, advanced towards the inevitable face-off at Actium in 31 B.C.

Meanwhile Virgil's life had changed. In Mantua, his father had died and his mother remarried. (She had a child by the new marriage whom Virgil much later remembered generously in his will.) Pollio, with his Antonian connections, was gone. Octavian generously offered Virgil land in the South, successively in the Naples area, in Rome, and in Sicily. So the poet left his family farm—so far as we can tell, never to return. As part of Octavian's circle, Virgil became a close friend of the slightly younger poet Horace. Maecenas, Octavian's cultural advisor, interested him in a new project—a larger-scaled Alexandrian genre, the didactic poem. This was to become the *Georgics,* another kind of journey backward in memory to the Mantua farm, more realistic than the essentially metaphorical *Eclogues,* and much more supportive of Octavian.

Virgil then thought about publishing his individual eclogues as a collection, and arranged the nine of them in an order designed to please his new connections (with *Eclogue* 1, on Octavian's merciful treatment of the Mantuans, at the start and *Eclogue* 5, on the deification of Julius Caesar, at the center), and to express as well his continuing pessimism (with *Eclogue* 9, on the dispossessed, at the close).

Eclogue 10 was added sometime later, as an afterthought, a postlude. It was written for, and perhaps at the request of, Gallus, at some crisis in that promising young man's dizzying career.[12] Gallus eventually paid less attention to poetry, where he seemed destined for greatness, than to politics, where he came to be recklessly ambitious. Virgil, who had proclaimed the potential greatness in *Eclogue* 6, all but predicts the unfortunate end in *Eclogue* 10.

Virgil was more fortunate than most of his contemporaries. He must have been shaken by what happened in Mantua. We do not need the unsubstantiated story in the fourth-century commentary by Servius (that he fell out with the soldier who claimed his farm, and only saved his life by leaping into the Mincius[13]) to believe that the

Eclogues were written out of personal experience, that they saved
the poet in a time of trouble. Like many poets since, Virgil used the
pastoral's ideal landscape as a solace for pain and also as a
preliminary experiment, as a prelude for writing greater works. In
the *Eclogues,* an Alexandrian miniaturist with more talent than
perhaps he knew, a sensitive young man who—to put it
insensitively—had had a bellyfull of history, turned to a book two
centuries old, and selected passages from it to express his own
sorrows, fears, feelings of gratitude, and hopes for the future.

When the *Eclogues* were published they were an immediate
success, not just with the literary circles that could appreciate their
studied refinement and their allusions to high-placed political
figures, but with the public at large. Donatus tells us[14] that they
were sung and mimed in theaters—an adaptation that Virgil could
hardly have anticipated when he made them so subtle. He probably
expected only to stimulate minds and imaginations; he appears also
to have touched hearts: Tacitus reports (*Dialogues* 13) that during
one of the public performances the shy and retiring Virgil was
present, and the crowd rose spontaneously in tribute. This might
have been in deference to a young poet who had successfully
rendered in Latin an elusive Greek Alexandrian art form; it was
more likely in honor of a man who had caught up everyone's recent
history in a poetic instant and preserved it. He had given the
permanence of art to the ordinary man's sufferings in the civil
wars, and expressed the hopes of all Italians for a peaceful future.
They were grateful.

Virgil set his *Eclogues* only partly in Theocritus' Sicily and
only partly in his own troubled Mantua. As he kept writing he came
to blend Sicily and Mantua in a new landscape of his own
imagining, Arcadia. And to that land we now turn.

IV

Arcadia

"Arcadia was discovered in the year 42 or 41 B.C." So
begins one of the most influential essays written on Virgil in our
century."[1]

Of course Arcadia, the land-locked, mountainous area in the
center of the Peloponnese, "had always been known," but was
seldom thought of. Greek civilization hardly touched it. This
geographic Arcadia remained cut off by mountains, remote and
primitive. It hardly cared that, in the days when Athens and then
Alexandria busied themselves with making works of art out of
myth, it could lay claim to being, in myth, the oldest land on earth.

In myth, Arcadia had always existed. Its people were older
than the moon. Its first ruler, Pelasgus, grew out of the ground. Its
first inhabitants were similarly autochthonous, born like acorns out
of a mother oak. Acorns in fact became their food. They hunted
and herded. On mountain tops they worshipped Pan, the son of
Hermes, god of herds, half-goat himself. They prayed he would
appear to them, horns on his head, his face smeared with red
mulberry juice so they could look on him without being harmed. At
the dawn of time, on Mt. Maenalus, he had taught them the art of
playing the pipe, which was his own invention. His music became
their solitary art.

If ever there was a primeval age of oneness with nature, the
Arcadians must have known it. So the story had to be told that one
of them committed man's original sin. The sin of their king
Lycaeus is variously reported as ritually sacrificing one of his own
children; as trying to trick Zeus into partaking of the flesh; as
trying, when he had Zeus as guest, to kill him by night. The
cross-references to Tantalus and Prometheus are clear enough. In

punishment Lycaeus was turned by Zeus into a wolf (*lycos*), and the wolf came to be the totem animal of primitive Arcadia.

The quite different Arcadia that was discovered in 42 or 41 B.C. never existed, on the map or even in myth, until Virgil found it in his imagination.[2] There it sometimes looked like his own Mantua, sometimes like Theocritus' Sicily, sometimes like the real Arcadia so long ignored. But it is, symbolically, all the world. It casts man in the role of shepherd, whose simple life becomes the ideal which every man, grappling with the complexities of human experience, could wish for himself.

We can glimpse Arcadia at the start of any one of the *Eclogues*,[3] but its fascination begins to take hold only when we have lived in the poems and wondered about them. Then it never quite lets go. For anyone who surrenders, Arcadia will be, as it was for one Englishman, "vividly realized for a moment," and then "the light tends to shimmer, shift and waver." The figures on the landscape "dissolve mysteriously or melt into something else." Sometimes only the foreground is visible, then again we are granted "distant views of astonishing brilliance and luminosity; but soon the curtain of mist closes again, dazzling but unfathomable. In this trance-like landscape most worldly values become such stuff as dreams are made on."[4]

Just as we are never sure, in this landscape, whether we are in Sicily or Mantua or the geographical Arcadia, so we are never sure whether the figures we see are supposed to represent the poet-statesmen Pollio or Varus or Gallus, or other poets who know no matters of state, or then again no one in particular. Sometimes Pollio and Varus are addressed outside the context of the poems, and Gallus actually appears, first within a narrative, then in his own person, walking in Roman armor in this imaginary shepherd's landscape. We cannot really tell whether the mourned Daphnis is Julius Caesar, or the new god receiving the shepherds in Rome Octavian. The many competitors in rustic song may be Virgil's contemporaries Varius and Cinna and Tibullus, or his predecessors Theocritus and Callimachus and Catullus, or his own self. Virgil seems to be one shepherd here, and yet another there, and then again neither. The feeling is fluid. We are invited, always, to wonder who is who, even though we know there are no fixed answers. Above all we are invited to ask, "What else does it mean?" For Arcadia is a metaphor.

When we glimpse it first, it looks like Virgil's father's farm. Here, in *Eclogue* I, are the beeches, the apple trees, the pear trees, the vines, the ploughlands, the cattle and goats, the hazel thickets, the willow hedges alive with bees, the dove cooing in the elm, the nearby hills casting long shadows across the turfed cottages, the chimneys smoking. A perfect land but, like Mantua's three-mile zone, it is circled round with shingle and marsh, mud and reeds, and, as the neighboring farmers are evicted, shadows begin to spread across it.

In *Eclogue* 2, as the sun rises again and bakes the countryside, we can see another, larger villa, with fields ready for harvesting. By noon the cattle have sought the shade, the lizards the undergrowth, the cicadas the orchard trees. The farm faces higher hills, covered with forest. There you might go hunting for deer or, in a valley, find two little white-spotted chamois. There you might even see—but be careful he does not see you—the god Pan. In this Sicily or Mantua or Arcadia? Before we can tell, the sun is setting, lengthening the shadows.

Next, as the sheep graze onwards, we come in *Eclogue* 3 to a crossroads, a shrine, and the strawberry fields and flowering banks of what must be the Mincius. But can we be sure this is Mantua? For *Eclogue* 4 invites us to leave the tamarisks of Sicily, in imagination at least, and anticipate the return of the Golden Age. Then in *Eclogue* 5 we begin again amid Mantua's hazels and elms and move to a cave overhung with vines that may very well be Sicily again, for the cave speaks of the Sicilian Daphnis.

In *Eclogue* 6, we hear of another cave, the haunt of fauns and nymphs, fronting on valleys and surrounded by stout oaks—Arcadia, perhaps? Before we can tell, the starry night comes on and, in the morning of *Eclogue* 7, we see Mantua's Mincius once more, though the shepherds contesting on its banks are called "Arcadians, both". Then, in *Eclogue* 8, the scene is suddenly a primitive forest, where heifers and lynxes alike are stunned by beautiful songs; where they know of both Mt. Maenalus in land-locked Arcadia and of Sicily's sea, into which a lover can plunge from high cliffs to his death; where one herdsman sings of an apple orchard all enclosed, a place of virginal innocence, and another sings of an uninnocent cottage where an enchantress casts spells.

The threat of rain hangs over the land in *Eclogue* 9, and as the night comes on again in the distance we can see a tomb. It seems like Theocritus's island of Cos, but the speakers and the tomb are Mantuan. Beyond all this, in *Eclogue* 10, lie the high Alps north of Mantua, with their dizzying crags and endless snows and, beyond them still, the frosted Rhine—or are those slopes really in Arcadia? Are they the sides of Mt. Lycaeus weeping still for the world's first sin, or of the mad mountain, Maenalus? Then again, the slopes might be those of Sicily's Etna, for it is the Sicilian nymph, Arethusa, who is helping us remember this last of the poems. Finally, as the goats make for home and the evening star appears, one last time the shadows cover everything again.

What is this Arcadia? If it is a true metaphor it must mean, not one, but several things.[5] It is, first, a place half-way between a past dimly remembered in myth, a Golden Age of innocence, and the troubled present. It is "a middle country of the imagination,"[6] the present once removed, the present set at a distance so that it can be dealt with and lived through. Arcadia is also a place of self-discovery. A poet may test himself there, confront himself amid images of love, life, suffering, and death, divide himself into two or three or more imaginary persons, or speak in his own person from outside the vision. As he projects himself, or aspects of himself, onto an imagined landscape, a poet sensitive to his own hopes, doubts, fears, and desires can objectify them and make his purposes clear in his own eyes.[7]

It is possible, then, to say that in this composite picture of a past tradition (Sicily), a personal experience (Mantua), and a mythic memory of primeval innocence ended by an original sin (Arcadia), in this newly fashioned, metaphorical Arcady, everything has symbolic value. If shepherds can be poets, then sheep can be their poems, and cattle, goats, birds and bees stand for varieties of genre. Vines to be tended and apples to be plucked can be poetic ideas yet unshaped or unrealized.[8] Rivers then will be sources of inspiration, caves mouths of oracular utterance, forests the dark unconscious. Mountains will signify limits set to artistic activity. The whole landscape can weep or rejoice with the figures that make poetry in the little pictures it provides. The sun can signify the memory of the Golden Age that still makes poetry possible till the shadows come on. Birth can mark the creation, and death the end, of poetry. Apotheosis can mean poetry's re-appearance, its rebirth, in some higher form.

It is possible to say all this, and yet the symbols remain, inviting further explanation and defying it, ever elusive.

V

Figures in a Landscape

Who are the figures that appear in Virgil's elusive
Arcadia, and what might they represent?

We can recognize many of them from Theocritus. There, in
Eclogue 9, still walking across the landscape but now walking
towards the city, not from it, is the mysterious Lycidas, whose
name, "son of the wolf," now suggests that he comes from the
wilds of primitive Arcadia. He is sadder now, but still a singer
intent on exchanging songs with the wayfarers he meets. There too,
in *Eclogue* 3, we see again Theocritus' young Damoetas ("the
people's choice"), competing in song as before, and tieing again
with his opponent. There, in *Eclogue* 7, is Theocritus' skilled
singer Thyrsis ("he of the Bacchic wand"), perhaps too brashly
over-confident in his Latin reappearance.

Names familiar from the *Idylls* recur: Amyntas ("the
contestant") is still impossibly handsome and, as befits his name,
much more intent now on song competitions; Antigenes ("aris-
tocrat") still prompts admiration; Aegon ("goat-fold") still owns
flocks, and Micon ("short-statured") vineyards; Neaera ("nether
region"?) still has something of the courtesan about her, while
Alcippe ("with the strength of a horse") still does farming tasks,
and Thestylis ("she who sets the table"?) prepares herbs as before.

We hear of gods familiar from Theocritus, fitted now with
Latin names—the Olympians Jupiter, Ceres, Venus, Apollo and
his sister Diana. Arethusa, Theocritus' freshwater nymph who
preserved her true nature when she swam through the salt sea from
Arcadia to Sicily, is invoked by Virgil when, at the end of the
Eclogues, he has completed something like the reverse journey. We
also hear of Theocritus' fertility god Priapus and, very briefly, we

see Pan, the Arcadian forest god, horned and hoofed, capable in his visitations of spreading panic, but benevolent in *Eclogue* 10, smeared red with minium and elderberries, and with fauns and satyrs in his train.

Two of his young fauns, Chromis ("color") and Mnasyllus ("remembering the forest"), we may not know from other contexts,[1] but surely we know, from many passages in Greek poetry and prose, Silenus, the Socrates-like satyr the two fauns find, ugly but wise, in an oracular cave in *Eclogue* 6. Among the fresh-water nymphs who haunt Virgil's land, Aegle ("the gleaming one") also comes to Silenus' cave to hear his marvelous song. Finally, there are Virgil's Italian gods — Pales, the androgynous god of agriculture, and Silvanus the forest god, with his headdress of fennel and lilies waving on their stalks.

Then there are human figures new with Virgil: Palaemon ("wrestler"), who judges a rough-and-ready song contest; Iollas ("violet-crowned"?) who owns property and seems to extend proprietary rights over his lovers as well; and Codrus (with connections in pre-historic Athens?) who sings like Apollo and is the envy of the other singers. We hear the songs of Damon ("the singer of popular songs"?), who sings perhaps the most beautiful song ever sung, of Alphesiboeus ("he who wins in competition"), who competes with Damon, and of young Mopsus ("freckle-faced"?), ready to mate with Nysa ("tree-like?), and very good at singing but impatient with the mastersinger he competes with — until he hears the mastersong.

Perhaps ten figures should be singled out for special mention. Foremost of these is the one the freckle-faced Mopsus sings of. He has died in the midst of a *locus amoenus*. He is DAPHNIS ("laurel"), the subject of the very first *Idyll* of Theocritus, and the archetypal figure for the whole pastoral tradition.[2] Child of Hermes and a Sicilian water nymph, exposed in infancy under a laurel tree, lovingly nurtured by nature and then by a herdsman, Daphnis grew up to be a herdsman himself, the best in all Sicily at singing. But (as we reconstruct the details of his myth from references scattered among many authors) he incurred the enmity of the love god Eros when he vowed everlasting fidelity to a nymph. Eros spitefully caused him to feel desire for a mortal woman, who seduced him with a love potion and abandoned him. The nymphs then blinded

him for breaking his vow. So, when we meet Daphnis in
Theocritus's first *Idyll,* he defies Eros' mother Aphrodite and dies
calling on nature to witness the injustices done him.

Virgil uses some of these details to create, almost impressionistically, a Daphnis who after death becomes a god. If we read the
Eclogues in sequence, Daphnis is first[3] a young herdsman who is
not only beautiful (*Eclogue* 2) but something close to Amor (Eros)
when his bow and arrows are smashed (*Eclogue* 3). Then in
Eclogue 5, he is remembered after his death as a hero, riding like
Bacchus in a chariot drawn by tigers. His death also has about it
something of the mythic significance that attaches to Adonis and
Attis, even to Osiris and Tammuz: he dies in the arms of his
mother, is taken to Olympus, and is worshipped on earth as a god.
He becomes, like those other figures, a symbol of the yearly death
and rebirth of nature, which weeps at his passing and shouts for joy
at his apotheosis. It is hard, too, to dismiss the thought that,
historically speaking, Virgil might intend the dying Daphnis to
stand for Julius Caesar, and the restored and benevolent Daphnis
for Octavian. For, if we read *Eclogue* 7 right, Daphnis returns to
earth, a god in epiphany under an ilex tree,[4] drawing the shepherds
and flocks to him, rescuing the unfortunate herdsman who was
evicted in the land confiscations.

We see Daphnis, then, in many different ways, wondering
always who or what he is supposed to represent. In the final
eclogues we remember him in two songs, in the love-mad woman's
incantation in *Eclogue* 8 and in the sadly half-forgotten hymn in
Eclogue 9. Is the first meant to be the song of one of the fatal
women in his myths, and is the second meant to express Virgil's
pessimism about history's future under Octavian? Virgil keeps us
guessing.

Almost as famous in the pastoral tradition is TITYRUS
("satyr" or "piper"). His is the first name, indeed the first word, in
the *Eclogues*—hence the entire collection has come to be called
"Tityrus". He is a little old man, utterly self-absorbed, piping
beneath a beech tree in *Eclogue* 1—happy because the sea nymph
Galatea, a venal sort, has finally left him, and he has found a new
love, Amaryllis, who has encouraged him to save his money; and
happy, too, because in the great city, Rome, a godlike young man
has saved his farm for him while others have been evicted.

Elsewhere, as in Theocritus, Tityrus is the one to call on when your goats need tending (*Eclogues* 3 and 9), though he is clearly absent-minded, and certainly no Orpheus or Arion at making music (*Eclogue* 8).

Who is this Tityrus? Ever since the fourth-century commentator Servius he has been thought to be Virgil himself, saved from eviction by order of the godlike young Octavian. But why, if that is so, is he cast as a simpleton, and why does his beard "fall white beneath the shears?" On the other hand, when Virgil is speaking in his own person in the introduction to *Eclogue* 6, why does he represent Apollo as calling him Tityrus? As with the landscape, so with the figures on it—the feeling is fluid.[5]

Virgil might as easily be, and again as easily not be, the gradually maturing figure MENALCAS ("abiding strength"). In Theocritus, Menalcas tended his father's sheep, and that is the way he appears in Virgil, too. In *Eclogue* 2 he is a boy, "dark but beautiful". In *Eclogue* 3 he is able to hold his own, like Gavin Maxwell's fifteen-year-old Sicilian, in exchanges of abuse and amoebean song; he is sexually precocious, destructive, contemptuous but not, given his age and what we know of such songs, contemptible. In *Eclogue* 5 he has matured, mastered his singer's art, and found gentleness and tact in his exchanges with the hot-headed but promising young Mopsus, who ends up praising him lavishly—and no wonder, for among the songs Menalcas has by heart are *Eclogues* 2 and 3 (hence his identification, for some, with Virgil). In *Eclogue* 9 things have gone badly for Virgil-Menalcas: he has tried to save the farms in the land from being taken over by aliens, and has barely escaped with his life; until he returns to the landscape it will be difficult for the other shepherds, who can only recall parts of his songs, to sing. Then, suddenly, in *Eclogue* 10 he is back, an Arcadian "still wet from steeping his winter store of acorns," as Virgil leaves Arcadia forever.

Of Arcadia's ladies the most delectable is PHYLLIS ("flourishing"), who is desired by no less than five different shepherds in *Eclogues* 3, 5, and 7, by the Roman Gallus in *Eclogue* 10, and by Jupiter himself in a song in *Eclogue* 7. Phyllis has in fact only to approach and—as with Handel's Semele—the trees put forth green leaves and Jupiter sends a full, happy shower from the sky. (Congreve eliminated the brasher sexual element of this when he wrote the words for "Where'er you walk.") Phyllis was never mentioned in Theocritus and never actually appears in Virgil, for all that she is spoken of and desired.

Also only spoken of in Virgil is GALATEA ("milk-white"). Her vain coquetries have done Tityrus out of all his savings in *Eclogue* 1. She throws apples flirtatiously and runs to hide behind the willows in the song in *Eclogue* 3, and the things she says when caught the winds might carry to the ears of the gods. She is called whiter than a swan in *Eclogue* 7, and in *Eclogue* 9 a shepherd sings a snatch, in Latin, of *Idyll* XI, which clearly identifies her as the sea-nymph wooed, in Theocritus, by the monster Polyphemus.

AMARYLLIS ("casting glances"), ever beautiful in Theocritus, is less consistent but far more fascinating throughout Virgil's collection. She has replaced Galatea in old Tityrus' affections in *Eclogue* 1 and seems—or at least he thinks her—a gentle sort. But from what is said in *Eclogues* 2 and 3 she has been moody and sulky with other lovers, and though in *Eclogue* 9 she seems to have been everyone's mistress, in *Eclogue* 8 it is Daphnis she loves obsessively, trying with the aid of an enchantress to conjure him to her cottage. Is she the nymph in the old Daphnis myths to whom he swore fidelity? Or is she the human girl who gave him the love potion and forced him to break his vow? Virgil leaves the matter open, and Amaryllis remains a name to conjure with.

CORYDON ("lark" or "hazel"), a hired man in Theocritus, is still pruning the master's vines and herding the master's sheep in Virgil—when he remembers to. His rustic mind is not on his work because, after his love affairs with brilliant Amaryllis and dark Menalcas, he has fallen hopelessly and somewhat comically in love with his master's favorite, the city-bred boy Alexis. Corydon imagines the boy hunting and piping with him in the woods, accepting baskets of flowers, living in idyllic bliss. And though neither nature nor Alexis ("he who doesn't reply") respond to his song in *Eclogue* 2, the luckless Corydon has a poet's vivid imagination and a good ear for sound, and in *Eclogue* 7 he defeats in song the skilled but over-confident Thyrsis.

MOERIS ("the grieving one" or "the fated one" or "the one who is half") is not to be found in Theocritus' Sicily but, given

Virgil's interest in supernatural motifs, belongs naturally in the Virgilian Arcadia. He is a warlock able to change himself into a wolf and vanish in the forest, to call up ghosts from their graves, to shift whole harvests from one field to another, to travel as far as the Black Sea for his magic herbs—or is all of this simply the raving of the enchantress in *Eclogue* 8? In *Eclogue* 9, warned by the cry of a raven from a hollow oak, he has saved his life and that of Menalcas from the brutal soldiers of Rome but, frightened by a pack of wolves (the Roman soldiers?), he has lost his voice and forgotten his spells. He has also lost his property in the confiscations. Grown powerless and old, driving his flock to their new owner, he walks ruefully onwards towards the city as night comes steadily on, speaking with the mysterious Lycidas, the wolf-son, trying to remember the songs of Menalcas, whom he has lost. With the aspect of the wolf clinging to him, with his curious symbiosis with Menalcas never fully explained, the grieving, fated, half-man Moeris is the most intriguing of all the figures on the landscape.

The figure who most speaks for the evicted is the eloquent MELIBOEUS ("sweet-crying" or "concerned for his flock"). In *Eclogue* 1, as he drives his flock into exile, he weeps some of the most beautiful lines in the collection. In *Eclogue* 3, the young shepherds do not know where his flock is. But in *Eclogue* 7, the risen Daphnis appears in epiphany and calls Meliboeus and his flock safely back to the river Mincius, to witness the song contest of Corydon and Thyrsis.

The figure the world knows best from the *Eclogues* has no name at all. He is the divine child in *Eclogue* 4, the PUER soon to be born amid ivy and foxglove, lily and acanthus. His advent will mark the gradual return of the long-lost, half-remembered Golden Age, when the serpent will die, the animals live in peace with one another, and the earth spontaneously produce its bounty.

The hero-child of undiscovered parentage, protected by nature and preserved by shepherds, is a figure as mythic as Oedipus, as old in Roman tradition as Romulus and Remus, still familiar in later ages in Shakespeare's *Winter Tale*. Something of his archetypal quality can be found in the widely separated myths of the young Moses, Siegfried, and King Arthur. And, as Virgil invests his child with details that sound like the prophecies of Isaiah, a long Christian tradition from Constantine through St.

Augustine to Dante and Pope has harbored the thought that Virgil, whose writings seemed through the centuries increasingly prophetic of events in Christendom, was predicting in the descent of his *puer* from heaven the birth of Christ. *Eclogue* 4 became the "Messianic Eclogue," and Virgil's child who will "recognize his mother with a smile" was identified with the child of Mary laid among the animals and adored by shepherds.

Virgil almost certainly had access to various near-Eastern wisdom literatures.[6] But he also had a precedent for this divine child in Theocritus' non-pastoral *Idyll* XVII, wherein the island of Cos receives the new-born Ptolemy from his mother's arms with a cry of gladness and an omen from on high. It is in fact as easy to read *Eclogue* 4 historically as it is to read it messianically. Though it is much more than a mere encomium like Theocritus' idyll, Virgil was careful to provide in it historical details sufficient to enable the powerful of his day to read it as an encomium, and apply it to themselves, if they so wished: Octavian, Antony, and Pollio all fathered children at the time of its composition.

The weight of internal evidence, especially the placing of the poem in the year when Pollio was consul and effected the Peace of Brundisium between Octavian and Antony, would seem to point to Pollio's expected child as the *puer* to be born. But as Julius Caesar was officially deified only two years earlier, the one family uniquely qualified to produce a divine child was the Julian. So either Octavian or Antony (newly married to Octavian's sister to cement the peace of Brundisium) could be the father of the expected divine child. Once again, Virgil leaves the matter open,[7] and the *puer* remains to this day one of the most controversial figures in all of literature.

It is time at last to summarize the subject matter of the *Eclogues*.

Eclogue 1: Tityrus, who has kept his land thanks to a godlike youth he has seen in Rome, engages in dialogue with Meliboeus, who has been evicted from his land by a ruthless soldier.

Eclogue 2: Virgil (addressing the reader) tells how the rustic

Corydon loved the boy Alexis, and repeats the lovesick song that neither nature nor Alexis listened to.

Eclogue 3: Menalcas and Damoetas, two young and not-quite-master poets, engage in a song competition with old Palaemon as judge, and with two pairs of cups or two heifers as prizes. They break even, and each is judged worthy of a heifer.

Eclogue 4: Virgil (addressing Pollio) sings that the Golden Age will return to earth at the impending birth of a baby boy, sent down from heaven (The "Messianic Eclogue").

Eclogue 5: Menalcas, much improved as a poet, retires to a cave with the younger Mopsus to sing of the death and apotheosis of the archetypal shepherd Daphnis.

Eclogue 6: Virgil (addressing Varus) tells how two young fauns caught the satyr Silenus in a cave. He then repeats the mythic song of creation and destruction that Silenus sang. In the midst of the myths, Gallus is commissioned by the Muses to write a new kind of poetry (The "Song of Silenus").

Eclogue 7: Meliboeus tells how Daphnis summoned him to witness the song competition between two very different master poets, Corydon and Thyrsis. Corydon wins.

Eclogue 8: Virgil (addressing Octavian) records two songs: Damon's of an innocent man who, unlucky in love, leaps to his death in water; Alphesiboeus' of a malicious woman who, unlucky in love, resorts to witchcraft with fire. The Muses dictate the second song.

Eclogue 9: Lycidas, who once confirmed Theocritus in his mission to sing, meets the dispossessed Moeris driving his flocks to their new owner in the city. The two try to recall the songs of their lost poet-protector Menalcas, and come upon a tomb. The future remains unclear.

Eclogue 10: Virgil (addressing the nymph Arethusa) tells how Gallus, unlucky in love, was welcomed in Arcadia like the dying Daphnis, but was unable to survive there. Virgil ends his singing and leaves Arcadia.

Clearly some of the figures in the *Eclogues* are closer to the imaginary landscape, farther from history, than others, and it will be helpful at this point to make some distinctions.[8] First there are the traditional pastoral figures, who may at most signify different kinds of poetry. Among these are the female figures (Galatea and Amaryllis provide quite different experiences for the poet Tityrus), and the herdsmen in competition (Menalcas and Damoetas are novices at poetry in *Eclogue* 3; Corydon and Thyrsis are Apollonian and Dionysian in their opposed poetics in *Eclogue* 7; Damon and Alphesiboeus sing, respectively, songs of unhappy and happy endings in *Eclogue* 8). Secondly there are the figures who, from suggestions of the poet himself, we are invited to see at least partly as historical personages—Daphnis (Julius Caesar and Octavian), Tityrus (Virgil, or at least those exempted from the land confiscations), Meliboeus and Moeris (those not exempted), Menalcas (Virgil again), and the *puer* (the child of Octavian, Antony, or Pollio). Thirdly there are the political personages addressed in their own names (Pollio, Varus and Octavian), and the contemporary poets mentioned approvingly (Varius and Cinna) or disapprovingly (Bavius and Mevius). A final figure is unique among them all. Happily placed somewhere between the imaginary landscape and the historical world in *Eclogue* 6, and tragically caught between them in *Eclogue* 10, is the gifted and doomed Gallus.

It will be seen from this summary that Virgil stands slightly apart from the figures on his landscape. He speaks in his own person in every second poem, briefly setting the scene and introducing the characters (*Eclogue* 2), addressing Pollio (*Eclogue* 4), Varus (*Eclogue* 6), Octavian (*Eclogue* 8), and the nymph Arethusa in concern for Gallus (*Eclogue* 10). Commentators have noticed, however, that he does not speak in the way that, say, Catullus and Horace do. He gives himself "almost no identity at all save what he acquires as the maker of his book."[9] This is altogether proper, for the pastoral is not the lyric; it is not a genre in which an artist reveals himself directly or through a clearly assumed persona. The pastoral is, as ancient critics thought it, a subspecies of epic: the poet is a narrator and an observer.

The distinction is important. In the *Eclogues* Virgil is not revealing himself so much as observing himself. Perhaps the best way to see Tityrus and Meliboeus in *Eclogue* 1 is to see them as two Virgilian attitudes—gladness for those who could keep their farms, sadness for those who could not. Perhaps the best way to see Corydon and Thyrsis in *Eclogue* 7 is to see them as two artistic options open to Virgil—the Apollonian and the Dionysian. In other poems, the constantly re-appearing Menalcas can be a figure for Virgil's gradually developing talent, Corydon of that talent's roots in a bi-sexual nature, Moeris of its vulnerable but real prophetic quality. Daphnis can represent Virgil's preoccupation (stronger still in the *Georgics* and *Aeneid*) with death and rebirth. The *puer* may signify the promise eventually to be realized in Virgil's mature work.

Who are the figures in the landscape? To some degree they are pastoral characters familiar from Theocritus and made to stand for historical personages in Virgil's experience. But to a degree more than is commonly thought, they can be figures for aspects of Virgil himself.

VI

Music: Eclogues 3 and 7

The historian Polybius was a native of Arcadia—the place on the map, not the imaginary landscape. He wrote of it (*Histories* 4.21.2) as a land so bleak and unproductive that the Arcadians took to song to make their lives bearable; even from childhood they cultivated the art of singing, and sang poems of their own composition in contests.

Virgil's composite Arcadia, a much more agreeable place, carries on the other Arcadia's tradition of musical competition. All of Virgil's shepherds are poets who sing their poems (even the dispossessed Meliboeus and Moeris once sang like the others). Five of the *Eclogues* are dialogues, and *Eclogues* 3 and 7 are examples of that special kind of dialogue called amoebean, in which the challenger sets the theme, meter, image-pattern and language, and the challenged attempts in every response to improve on his opponent—refuting, contrasting, going him one better (and often, if losing, actually winning in subtle ways[1]). "Then there's songs you sing in alternate verses," says Gavin Maxwell's young Sicilian, instinctively carrying on the tradition in our century. As one of Virgil's shepherd-judges says, "The Muses love these songs that go back and forth": *amant alterna Camenae*.

The sounds in that very phrase, *amant alterna Camenae*, show Virgil's way with word-music. Five (or, with the diphthong, six) assonant *a*'s are floated on a series of liquid consonants—*m* and *n* at the ends of the phrase, *l* and *r* at the center. Two percussive t's punctuate the pattern. That leaves only the solitary *c* otiose—or is the *c* rather the sound we hear clearest, heightened as it is by the surrounding patterns?

Alexander Pope, a man not given to sentimental exaggeration, said of the *Eclogues* that they were "the sweetest poems in the world." "Sweet" is not the first adjective most commentators, impressed with Virgil's complexity, would give the poems today. But "sweet" *is* the first word in the first idyll of Virgil's predecessor Theocritus, and no Greek ever wrote a more ear-alerting opening than his

> hády ti tó psithyrísma kai há pitys, aípole, téna

> Sweet is the whispering sound of the pine tree there, my goatherd.

In their sound-patterns, Virgil's Theocritan poems might indeed be "the sweetest poems in the world." Take the first lines of the first Eclogue, spoken by the appropriately named "sweet-crying" Meliboeus to the happy Tityrus:

> Tityre, tu patulae recubans sub tegmine fagi
> silvestrem tenui Musam meditaris avena;
> nos patriae finis et dulcia linquimus arva.
> nos patriam fugimus; tu, Tityre, lentus in umbra
> formosam resonare doces Amaryllida silvas.

The opening *Títyre tú* is instantly alliterative and almost surely intended to call to mind and ear the *hády ti tó* of Theocritus' opening. In addition, it is balanced, in a long chiasmus of sound, by the *tu Tityre* in line 4. Within this frame are *nos patriae finis* (line 3) and *nos patriam fugimus* (line 4), and within that alliterative frame there is the delicate phrase *dulcia linquimus arva:* here the central sounds of *dulcia* are repeated in *linquimus* (*u-l-c-i* become *l-i-q-u*), and the final *a* of *dulcia* is picked up in the concluding *arva*. The liquid sound of the phrase is a subtle progression from labial (*l,l*) to dental (*n,m*) to the trilled *r*. (If, as is sometimes said, Romans could trill *l* as well as *r*, the phrase could certainly be spoken trillingly on the tongue.)

But there is more still within the *Tityre tu. . . tu Tityre* chiasmus. The *re* in *Tityre* is soon picked up in *recubans*. The *patulae* evokes Theocritus' *psitheri-*. The initial letters in *sub tegmine* are picked up in *silvestrem tenui*. *Musam meditaris* is an obvious alliteration. *avena* is close in sound to *arva* (*n* and *r* are both liquids). And perhaps the subtlest pattern is in line 2's *silvestrem . . . meditaris*, where the *s-i-t-r-e-m* of the first word is repeated anagramatically as *m-e-i-t-r-s* in the second.

The most beautiful line, however, is the fifth. Commentators have remarked on the resonant *o* in *formosam resonare doces*. But the vowel that determines the texture of the line is really *a*: within the frame provided by six *a*'s, the sound of the line passes from *ō* to *ŏ*, from *ĕ to ē,* to the thin *y* and *i*. The effect of this can best be heard by modern ears, often deaf to the niceties of such arrangements, when the line is spoken aloud in hexameter rhythm without the consonants:

ō-ō ā-ĕ-ŏ ā-ĕ-ŏ ē ă-ă- ȳ-ĭ-ă- ĭ-ă.

After that, perhaps the ear will be sensitized to hear the effect, around the vowels, of the eleven liquids and the five whispering sibilants. This is word-music of a high order.

Any page of the *Eclogues* would yield as much for the ear, as well as more obvious rhetorical effects. In the five lines that follow our passage we hear *deus nobis . . . ille . . . mihi semper deus illius . . . ille,* and the extraordinary

ludere quae vellem calamo
x   x ↓   xx x ↓ x x

where, undisturbed by sibilants, seven liquids prevail (*d* is the only consonant not working in the pattern). If, as Pope says, "the sound must be an echo of the sense," then perhaps Tityrus implies in this phrase that, now that he is restored to his land, there'll be no hissing, only mellifluous clarity in his peaceful piping.

Reading on in *Eclogue* 1, we hear simple alliterations (*miror magis; aeger ago),* alliterative patterns (*undique totis usque adeo turbatur agris,* with its *u-t-u-a-t-a; silice in nuda . . . saepe malum hoc nobis, si mens non,* with its patterned *s-n . . . s-m-n-s-m-n),* jingles both anagramatic (*permisit agresti)* and reinforced by ictus (*conixa reliquit).* Finally we can hear almost all of these phenomena, or acoustica, in the line

sed tamen ille deus qui sit da, Tityre, nobis.

Occasionally Virgil attempts a kind of rusticated Latin,[2] but nothing so flavorsome as Theocritus' stylized Doric. (Latin verse offered him no extensive use of dialects as a precedent, and realism was not, in any case, his aim.) He is more interested in preserving the metrical feel of his predecessor, using Theocritus' bucolic diaeresis (the break in the line after a fourth-foot dactyl) in two out of his five first lines. That percentage continues throughout most of the first *Eclogue,* reinforcing several of the phenomena we have already observed, and lending an almost abrupt emphasis to the affirmation in line 8 that the youth Tityrus has seen in Rome, a youth who almost surely represents Octavian, is a god:

nām-que ĕ-rĭt|īl-lĕ mĭ-|hī sēm-|pēr dĕ-ŭs‖īl-lĭ-ŭs|ā-răm.

Here the word *deus,* two short syllables in the arsis of a dactylic foot, is lifted and held by the diaeresis that follows.

Clearly Virgil is as happy making verbal songs as are any of his shepherds, but many of his happy shepherd's songs go sad. (*There* is a sentence written with Virgil's music still in the ears!) Music, sadly, is not the most potent force in Arcadia. Rocks and trees, animals and half-humans may all be shaken by Silenus' song in *Eclogue* 6, and mad Mount Maenalus may serve as "a sounding board"[3] for the loveless goatherd in *Eclogue* 8, but we note that only the first of these songs achieves its end: Silenus succeeds in revealing to his listeners the secrets of the world without and the world within, and the valleys toss his song to the stars; but the loveless goatherd gets no response, no solace for his pain, from Mount Maenalus, and falls to his death in the sea. Similarly Corydon's song in *Eclogue* 2 brings him no release from his passion: the mountains and forests do not answer. And Gallus in *Eclogue* 10 abandons pastoral verse when it does nothing to ease the torments of love. All of these songs that fail in their purposes succumb to a force that is greater than music—erotic passion. In the *Eclogues* passion can be and often is an obsession and an evil. And it is not the only evil: Meliboeus in *Eclogue* 1 can sing no more, and Moeris in *Eclogue* 9 has forgotten all his songs, because of the harsh realities of war. Eros and Ares constantly threaten Arcadia's singers—one from within them, the other from without.

Before we turn to the two poems that deal with music explicitly, we might ask whether there is any place in the *Eclogues* where Virgil provides us with a poetics, a set of standards for judging his carefully detailed, constantly threatened art. A.J. Boyle finds an *ars poetica* in the mostly metaphorical statements Virgil makes in the prologue, introduction, and narrative of *Eclogue* 6.[4] As the poet introduces the figure of Silenus, and then records how all nature responded to his song of the world's creation and impending destruction, Boyle finds six criteria for judging the worth of poetry:

> *(1) artistic control:* "A shepherd ought to feed his sheep fat and sing his song thin." (4–5; the maxim is from Callimachus)
>
> (2) *power to change the listener:* "Then you might have seen fauns and wild creatures playing in measure, and rigid oaks waving their heads." (27–8)
>
> (3) *a fertile union of both Apollonian and Dionysian,* of ordering intellect and daemonic inspiration: "Silenus, flushed with yesterday's Bacchus . . . sang all the songs that the river once heard from Apollo." (14–5; 82–4)
>
> (4) *creative force* analogous to that that shaped the world: "He sang how atoms were driven through the void . . . and all principles of life arose from them." (31–4)
>
> (5) *moral substance:* "He also sang of the sin of Prometheus and of the punishment dealt him on Caucasus." (42)
>
> (6) *compassion* that calls for compassion: "He sang how . . . all the shore resounded 'Hylas, Hylas!' (44)

Virgil's three major works can indeed be measured by these standards. His *Aeneid* may not be a "thin song," but it shows an artistic control, a careful patterning, that would have pleased Callimachus. His *Georgics* may seem to have nothing "Dionysian" about them—until the rending of Dionysian Orpheus at the close makes us re-think everything we have read. His *Eclogues* may seem at first to lack creative force, such is their delicacy, but they do "shape a world," and they serve as a beginning to the eventual fashioning of stronger stuff. About two other criteria, moral substance and compassion, there has never been, with Virgil, any doubt.

It is about the second of these standards—poetry's power to change, to transform the listener—that Virgil himself came to have doubts. In the very passage in which Boyle finds his six criteria, Virgil uses the word—*inanis*—which later came to express his pessimism about art and its power to change.[5] *Inane* is, in Silenus' song, the void out of which creation comes. It is also the word Virgil uses in *Eclogue* 2 of Corydon's useless attempt to persuade through song. And it is the lonely word he uses in the *Aeneid* when his hero sees a representation in art of his own sorrows and weeps over the *lacrimae rerum,* the sorrows of the world:

> atque animum pictura pascit inani.

> and he nurtured his soul on a picture that meant nothing.

Inanis—empty, futile, lifeless—is, as Adam Parry has taught us to see, an important word in the *Aeneid,* and an essential word in Virgil.[6] Though he never reached the point of saying that life was essentially meaningless, Virgil certainly thought, from the *Eclogues* onwards, that human nature was fundamentally flawed, and he grew to mistrust works of art that attempted to derive some meaning from or confer some meaning on human suffering, and so benefit humanity. Hermann Broch, in his massive, almost Proustian novel *The Death of Virgil,* has taken this a step further: Virgil despaired of his *Aeneid,* and wanted it destroyed, because he feared that the poem, intended as a criticism of empire, might be used as an instrument of imperial oppression; he also knew that no work of art could presume to say why the innocent suffer, or could compensate the sufferers for their suffering.

The beginnings of all of this are in the *Eclogues,* and may be observed even in the most optimistic of them, the "Messianic Eclogue": even when the Golden Age yellows the fields with waving wheat and makes the oaks drip honey, traces of some ancient sin *(sceleris vestigia nostri . . . priscae vestigia fraudis)* will linger on in us and send us to new wars. Similarly, in *Eclogue* 6 the "Song of Silenus" turns from the joyous creation of the world, and its recreation after the Flood, to a series[7] of myths in which mankind's punishment for the sin of Prometheus is perpetuated in the lives of the unfortunate figures Hylas, Pasiphae, the daughters of Proetus, the sisters of Phaethon, Atalanta, Scylla,

Tereus and Procne: traces of that original sin[8] continue to bring suffering and destruction.

Has any work of art the power to change the listener, to transform, to redeem? In the midst of the myths of man's degeneration in *Eclogue* 6, Virgil's Silenus introduces Gallus. The Muses call the young Roman from his wanderings in the valley of the Permessus (a symbol of love elegy) to Mount Helicon (where they once inspired Hesiod to sing the Greek myths of creation and original sin). At the top of the mountain, the Muses bestow on Gallus the very pipe on which Hesiod once played so persuasively that trees followed him down the mountain. The pipe is presented by the mythic Linus, symbol of fruition. The implication here, I would say, is that Gallus is to sing the myths of the race's creation and degeneration so persuasively that he will move and change mankind. But at the end of the *Eclogues,* Gallus seems to have failed in this mission (and, it was to turn out, failed in life as well, with his poems lost). By *Eclogue* 10, Virgil has learned in Arcadia that art does not always succeed in its high aims. It sometimes succumbs to other, more violent forces.

The preceding pages have, I think, been a necessary preparation to our consideration of the two amoebean eclogues, 3 and 7, that deal explicitly with the art of music, with what it can and cannot do.

In the light-hearted amoebean *Eclogue* 3, two works of art are described in some detail (though nowhere like the detail given by Theocritus in the corresponding part of *Idyll* I). Each young shepherd in a song competition has a pair of matching beechwood cups, never used, covered over with figures, that might be forfeit to the winner. Each could also put up as a prize a heifer rich with milk. One of the boys, Menalcas, would prefer to stake the cups because his parents count the flock every day and would miss the heifer at once; the other, Damoetas, would prefer to stake a heifer because his cups are carefully stowed away. Through the contest we are never quite sure what the prize will be.

The two sets of cups are, from their description, quite beautiful, carved by a master. Menalcas' cups show, beneath a clustering ivy vine, the figure of the astronomer Conon (the patron, in Alexandria, of Theocritus), and another figure Menalcas cannot remember—"he was the one who fixed all the dates whereby farmers do their work." (There are other possibilities, but we think that the unidentified figure could be Virgil, already looking forward to writing his *Georgics*.[9]) Damoetas' cups have, beneath acanthus leaves, Orpheus leading the trees with his song. (There are other possibilities, but we think that this figure might represent Virgil again, already contemplating Orpheus as his signature-figure in the *Georgics*.) The two pairs of cups suggest that man in touch with nature (beneath the leaves, leading the trees) can through science (Conon) make sense of, and through art (Orpheus) control, the world about him.

But the two shepherds, who before the contest cheerfully accuse each other of sodomy and sacrilege, of thieving and vandalism (remember Maxwell's contemporary cowherd and take the charges with a grain of Sicilian salt!), never really pass beyond Sicilian banter in the contest itself. Their exchanges are spirited and charming (much more so than some commentators would have it), but there is no indication that either of the boys knows what the figures on the cups might mean. Neither of them, in fact, has ever drunk from the cups.

The contest ends with an exchange of riddles. Damoetas asks Menalcas, "Tell me, and I'll think you as great as Apollo—where in the world is the space of the sky no more than three ells?" The answer seems to be "Wherever there is a planetarium with a telescope," but Menalcas, though his cups are adorned with astronomers' figures, seems not to know. He in turn asks Damoetas, "Tell me, and you can have Phyllis for your own— where in the world do flowers grow with kings' names on them?" The answer seems to be "Wherever grows the hyacinth, marked with the letters *ai* for King Aias in the *Iliad*," but Damoetas, though his cups are adorned with the poet and the trees, seems not to know.

The riddles remain unanswered.[10] The boys know nothing of the uses of art. The judge of the competition, Palaemon,[11] makes his decision only on the basis of the two boys' comments on love; each has known love's delights and pains, and so each deserves to win a heifer. Neither, presumably, is worthy of the cups. Works of art have never communicated any message to them.

Palaemon's is a Virgilian decision. The mass of humanity will find a live, productive animal of more use than any of man's lifeless artistic masterpieces; nature nourishing is more useful than nature intellectualized and ordered. Ultimately, Palaemon rewards the two boys only because each of them has shown, however briefly, some awareness of his human nature. But it is an awareness derived from experience, not from art.

The other amoebean contest, in *Eclogue* 7, is similarly set in a bright atmosphere—very bright indeed, if we think of Daphnis presiding under the ilex tree as the Daphnis whose death was sung of two eclogues back and who now appears like a god in epiphany; and if we think of Meliboeus at his side as the Meliboeus evicted in *Eclogue* 1, now rescued with all his herd; and if we think of Corydon singing as the lovesick Corydon of *Eclogue* 2, now free of his obsession. The contest in *Eclogue* 7 might them represent an occasion on which the power of music has for once triumphed over suffering and death.

The contest itself is a battle of wits between two master singers, introduced as equals *(pares)* and Arcadians both *(Arcades ambo)*. Gentle, imaginative Corydon will hang up his pipe forever if he loses. But in the event he rather handily wins over his opponent Thyrsis who, admittedly at a disadvantage by going second, seeks to win with realistic detail, sexual innuendo, and a bravado bordering on brashness. It is tempting to see the two different but equal Arcadians as the refined, muted, symbolic Virgil and the less reticent, more ebullient Theocritus, and the poem as a kind of *ars poetica*[12] (in which case it is charming of Virgil to dub his Sicilian predecessor an Arcadian). It is equally possible, and I think better, to see in the contest a pre-Nietzschean struggle between the Apollonian (Corydon's gods are Apollo, Diana, and the nymphs) and the Dionysian (Thyrsis, true to his name, invokes Bacchus and Priapus, and sees Jupiter only at his most orgasmic). Daphnis then is present because he is important to the art of each contestant, representing as he does something of both Apollo (herding the Sun's cattle in Stesichorus) and Dionysus (driving his tiger-drawn car in Virgil).

But Daphnis says nothing. It is the sweet-crying Meliboeus from *Eclogue* 1, a character who speaks at least partly for Virgil himself, who is called to witness the contest, and says at its end:

ex illo Corydon Corydon est tempore nobis.

The line can mean, not only "From that time on it was Corydon, Corydon for us shepherds," but "From that time on it was Corydon, Corydon within me." That is to say, each of the competitors in *Eclogue* 7 may represent an aspect (Apollonian and Dionysian) of Virgil himself. And the poem marks the poet's moment of decision.

Similarly, I think we shall see the speakers in *Eclogue* 1 — Tityrus and Meliboeus—as representing Virgil's happy and unhappy reactions to events in Mantua, and Menalcas and Moeris in *Eclogue* 9 as representing the outer and inner halves of the poet. In these poems, Virgil seems to be in dialogue with himself, dramatizing conflicting emotions, seeking self-understanding. *Eclogue* 7 is the most light-hearted of these, but the issue involved is serious. When he favors Corydon over Thyrsis Virgil chooses the former's gentler, subtler, Apollonian art. That, and not Thyrsis', is the music he will make his own.

VII

Love: Eclogues 2 and 8

"Virgil's shepherds are shepherds in love."[1] Damoetas loves Galatea, Menalcas loves Neaera, Mopsus loves Nysa, several shepherds of varying ages love Galatea, still more love Amaryllis, and just about everyone in Arcadia loves Phyllis. Nor is the grand passion always so heterosexual. Without any special comment from Virgil or any of the personages in his poems, Corydon loves the boy Alexis and wonders why he is more infatuated with him than with Menalcas. Iollas too loves Alexis, while Mopsus says he might have loved Antigenes. Further, promiscuity seems almost the norm: several shepherds claim to have had at least four separate lovers, indiscriminate of sex. And never do any of the loves lead to permanent relationships. The objective seems always to be sensual delight free from care, possibly even free from physical consummation—though that intruder in Arcadia, Silenus, certainly has something physical in mind when he promises, in *Eclogue* 6, a song for the two fauns who have asked for it and "a different reward" for the nymph who is with them.

If the one you love does not love you back, you find another— that is the Arcadian rule. The constant shepherd and the constant nymph are doomed to sorrow, for reciprocal love does not last in Arcadia, and unrequited love soon becomes a destructive obsession. Virgil's second *Eclogue* is concerned with this. Much of it might have inspired Marlowe's lines

> Come live with me and be my love,
> And we will all the pleasures prove
> That hills and valleys, dales and fields,
> And all the craggy mountains yields.

58

And much of it was, in turn, inspired by Theocritus' *Idyll* XI,[2] where the same pleading overtures were first put in the mouth of the monster Polyphemus as he attempts to woo the sea nymph Galatea. Virgil, between Marlowe and Theocritus, gives the time-honored words to the gentle shepherd Corydon.

Under the hot sun, Corydon is hotly, hopelessly in love with the boy Alexis, drawn to him as surely as the lion to the wolf, the wolf to the goat, the goat to the clover. Nature is cruel in the passion it implants in its creatures. And to compound the cruelty, the boy is possessed by Corydon's own master in the city, and cares not a whit for the shepherd's passion. Corydon sings his desire to the mountains and forests, hoping they will cast it on to Alexis, far away. He pleads with the boy to leave the city and live with him on the hills; he creates an imaginary world alive with delicious details. He also deludes himself into thinking that he himself is rich, handsome and talented. When the song is done, the sun is setting. Corydon has got no reply from Alexis *via* the mountains and forests. But he does not despair. His feelings are, we discover, keyed to the times of day: as the shadows fall, his passion subsides, and he consoles himself with his pastoral tasks.

Virgil has made Theocritus sad, but not sentimental. Both poets treat their unlikely lovelorn suitors with a delicate detachment: we neither laugh at them nor feel sorry for them. Each of the suitors finds, if not an answer, at least some relief after his song. Corydon will weave osiers and reeds into a basket, and find someone else to love.

Pastoral poetry—especially Virgil's which is woven from the osiers and reeds of Theocritus and others—is not lyric poetry. It is not written out of intense personal involvement in some romantic crisis. The truest lyric poet in Latin literature, Catullus, wrote love poems to the pseudonymous Lesbia out of his own experience. Horace, a lyric artist who could slip easily into the more relaxed role of epistolary satirist, wrote love lyrics to and about many pseudonymous girls and a few pseudonymous boys, but he kept everything distanced; it is impossible to say whether any of the loves in the poems corresponds to any real experience in Horace's personal life.[3] Some of the *Odes* of Horace, 1.5 and 1.22 for example,[4] seem to be saying beneath their surfaces that a lyric poet need not write intensely and immediately out of his own experience, and that it is safer not to do so. Horace may well have been right: he lived to almost twice Catullus' age. Poets who write intensely out of their personal experience seldom live long.[5] Catullus poured his most passionate feelings into the elegiac couplet and made that meter the vehicle for almost all subsequent Latin love lyric. Significantly, Horace never touched the couplet. His contemporaries who did—Tibullus with his elegiacs to "Delia" and Propertius with his to "Cynthia"—wrote out of, or in simulation of, personal involvement. Both died young.

Catullus and the elegists, then, represent a tradition in love poetry quite different from that in which Horace functioned. In the Catullan tradition, passion is immediate and real, or intended to be read as real. In the Horatian, passion, if it is expressed at all, is distanced, used almost symbolically.

Virgil, in *Eclogue* 2 and elsewhere, is closer to Horace. He is of course not writing lyric poetry at all, and no one looks to pastoral verse for the Catullan moment when the poet reveals himself. Virgil found the pastoral a vehicle for detached comment and, generally speaking, he left it that way. Horace approved. He said of the *Eclogues* that they were *molle atque facetum*— delicate and playful. He seemed to think them akin to his own stylized, unsentimental poems about Pyrrha, Leuconoë, Lalage, and Chloë.

But I like to think that Horace made his statement after reading only the early *Eclogues* 2 or 3, and that he found other adjectives for the others, when they appeared. For Virgil saw greater potential in the pastoral than did any of his predecessors. He was not incapable of intense feeling, and he certainly knew his Catullus. Sometimes, when he deals with love, moments of intense Catullan passion pierce through his delicately playful Horatian surfaces.

One such moment, which Voltaire thought the finest in Virgil and Macauley the finest in all of Latin, comes in *Eclogue* 8. An anonymous goatherd sings, before he leaps to his death:

saepibus in nostris parvam te roscida mala
(dux ego vester eram) vidi cum matre legentem.
alter ab undecimo tum me iam acceperat annus,
iam fragilis poteram ab terra contingere ramos:
ut vidi, ut perii, ut me malus abstulit error!

Within my family's enclosure, when you were a little girl,
I saw you gathering dewy apples with your mother.
(I was the guide for the two of you.)
The year after the eleventh had just come and taken hold of me.
I was just able, from the ground, to touch the tender branches.
One look, and that instant I died! That instant something evil
Took hold of me and bore me off, wandering and lost.

Like all great poetry, the lines almost defy translation. I've overtranslated *acceperat* and *abstulit* to point up their parallel positions and the special force of their prepositional prefixes. I've tried, clumsily perhaps, to convey the plural force of both *nostris* and *vester*. I've made much of *malus error,* though I've resisted the temptation to translate it "original sin" or "the knowledge that there is potential for evil in humankind," even if that is what the unexpected Latin words imply. I've simply ignored the difficulty in *ut . . . ut . . . ut* and settled for Page's old but excellent note on it, which I first read when twice the eleventh year had just taken possession of me. I've had to expand five marvelously compressed lines to seven. And finally, I've failed completely to convey the magical effect a Latin poet can, admittedly with some ease, achieve by word-placing. Virgil's details accumulate almost impressionistically: "in our enclosure . . . a little girl . . . you . . . dewy apples . . . I was your guide . . . I saw . . . with your mother . . . gathering."

"I cannot tell you how the lines struck me," writes Macauley. That is almost English for *ut vidi, ut perii!*

Some of Virgil's details here come from Theocritus, and marking the changes he makes will tell us much about Virgil's selective art. Theocritus (*Idyll* XI.26) says, "I fell in love with you, maiden, I did, on the day when you came with *my* mother, wanting to pluck *hyacinth blossoms* from the *mountainside,* and I led your way." It comes as something of a shock to discover that in Theocritus the passage is spoken by the one-eyed monster Polyphemus in his almost grotesque but strangely touching attempt to woo the sea nymph Galatea. Virgil has dared to take the passage from Theocritus, a passage his literate readers would certainly know, and know in its context, and use it in a new setting, to suggest the memory of lost innocence. In this he shows himself *mollis atque facetus*—delicate and playful—and a good deal more.

Virgil makes four changes in his selection, and he expects us to recognize and wonder about them. First, the two figures in the unequal love match are demythologized, changed from cyclops and sea nymph to boy and girl. And they are youthened: the *parvam te* and *alter ab undecimo . . . annus* neatly effect the transformation.

Second, the mother in Virgil's passage is not the boy's, but the girl's. This is clear from the Latin *vester*. Later in the poem we see the reason for this: "Now I know what love really is," the boy-grown-to-a-man laments. "He is a child not of our flesh and blood . . . and you, his mother, are cruel. Is the mother more cruel, or the wicked child? The child is wicked, but it is you, the mother, who are cruel." Virgil's goatherd now remembers that Love, too, is a child with a cruel mother. Like Eros and his mother Aphrodite, like Amor and his mother Venus, the girl-child and the mother who came into the apple-tree enclosure were the destroyers of his innocence.

Thirdly, the girl and her mother come, not for hyacinth blossoms, but for dewy apples. The hyacinth certainly has suggestive qualities, and a myth of its own. But Virgil needs a symbol of sexual awareness. That symbol, in Greek erotic poetry, in myth, and in literature to this day, is the apple. Laurie Lee called the chapter in which he remembers his sexual initiation "First Bite at the Apple": "Who can say—whatever disenchantment follows— that we ever forget magic, or that we can ever betray, on this leaden earth, the apple-tree." Similarly, Richard Llewellyn writes: "The tight-drawn branch is weak . . . Your eyes see plainly. The trees are green, just the same as they were . . . I had eaten of the tree. Eve was still warm under me . . . the smell of green, and the peace of the mountainside."[6]

These modern novelists have *Genesis* in mind, of course. Virgil, ever intuitive and archetypal, makes a fourth and most important change. Innocence is lost, not on a mountainside, picturesque as that may be (Llewellyn, we note, uses it). Virgil's scene is set *saepibus in nostris*—in a hedged-in enclosure, in a *saepes* private to the one whose innocence is lost. This is Virgil's most memorable use of what was to be called in pastoral the *locus amoenus,* the pleasance, "the green cabinet," the garden where man is one with nature, happy in his innocence. (A variant of this in the Middle Ages, the *hortus conclusus,* was a symbol of virginity, and a name given the Virgin herself.)

So Virgil has added, to Theocritus' original, the archetypal paradise and the archetypal apple familiar to the Western tradition from a wholly different culture. Perhaps this is why his pastorals came to be called eclogues or "selections"—so sensitive was he in selecting passages from his sources for his new, intuitive purposes.

Virgil completes the passage about the apple orchard with a line borrowed from a completely different poem of Theocritus, *Idyll* II. There, beneath the moon, an enchantress attempts by incantation to force the one she loves to love her. She remembers how she saw two youths walking side by side. "Their beards were more golden than the golden ivy blossom. Their breasts—they were coming from the wrestling ring where men become beautiful—were brighter even than your gleam, O Moon. One look, and that instant I went mad! That instant my heart was set afire." Virgil takes the last line of this, preserves the exact hexameter composition and even something of the sound (Theocritus' threefold *hos* goes neatly into Latin as a threefold *ut*), and applies it to his considerably different context. He knows full well that his readers will remember the original, and yet he takes the risk. He wants the line, not just for its love-at-first-sight despair, but for the idea of sight itself. Vision, insight, revelation was what he needed for his boy in the apple enclosure. Selecting from his Greek original, Virgil now has the word *vidi* twice—once from each Theocritan context—and a passage in which sight, or insight, is all-important.

Virgil's special insight—what his orchard-boy feels but does not quite articulate—is that our original sin myths (Prometheus and Pandora which Virgil knew, Eve and other near-Eastern myths which he only may have known) are myths not of sin so much as of the dawning of awareness, of consciousness, of seeing and knowing where before there was only innocent unknowing. Whether we think of primitive people as living a brutish cave-man's existence (as in Lucretius) or imagine them, from some mythic memory, as living in a paradise where all their wants are provided for by a loving, nurturing nature (as in *Genesis* and the Golden Age myth), the primitive man we imagine is unreasoning, unquestioning, simply surviving in nature's environ. He is one with nature, until he takes his most important evolutionary step—his emergence into consciousness.

It is a necessary step, this severing of his ties with nature, but in every mythology it brings with it a sense a guilt (perhaps expressed in an etymological link between sin or *Sünde* and sunder or *sondern*). What man thought was a *malus error* was an emergence into self-awareness. When Adam and Eve sinned they ate of the fruit of the tree of *knowledge*. They became aware of themselves. Unlike the animals who had no such consciousness, they sought to cover their nakedness, for they knew, from the apple in the enclosed garden, their potential for good and evil. They were indeed, as the tempter had promised, like gods, for man is godlike, not animal-like, when he knows himself. But forever after they felt guilty about their new evolutionary status and, driven out of the enclosed garden and having to labor thereafter to survive, they wept for the blissful time they knew before they had sundered the bond with nature, the time when they were idyllically innocent and unaware, with the animals.

The memory of this, so much a part of man's mythologies, is a memory every man and woman has in his or her own life, derived from the experience of passing from childhood to adulthood, derived most specifically in the moment when the young person first becomes aware of his or her sexual potential. With that flash of insight, everything changes, innocence is lost: *ut vidi, ut perii, ut me malus abstulit error!* In the shelter of the apple orchard, "the boy who bends the branches to offer the fruit is a giver of nature and love. Although the apples are a promise of amatory experience, he expects that such experience will always remain as innocent and undisturbing as in childhood."[7] Then suddenly he sees his nature in a wholly new way, as a *malus error*. The world becomes alien and wild to him.

Now the girl he fell in love with then, Nysa, is to marry another, Mopsus. The song the luckless full-grown goatherd sings is one last effort to persuade her to love him instead. It is punctuated by a refrain

> incipe Maenalios mecum, mea tibia, versus

> Begin, my pipe, to sing with me Maenalian verses

that has the force of an incantation. The refrain casts a spell. But the spell does not work, and the goatherd leaps into the sea. Or does he? Virgil only has him say:

> omnia vel medium fiat mare. vivite, silvae:
> praeceps aerii specula de montis in undas
> deferar; extremum hoc munus morientis habeto.

Let everything become mid-sea. Farewell, forests!
I'll be borne down headlong from the lookout of an aery rock
Into the waves. Let her have this last offering from me as I die.

How literally are we to take this? The dying man has repeatedly called his song *Maenalios versus*. Presumably it was sung on or to Mount Maenalus, in land-locked Arcadia. Nowhere in the Peloponnese is farther from the sea. Even granted that Virgil's Arcadia is an ever-shifting time-space continuum conjured up only partly from the actual Arcadia, a Maenalian leap into the sea is an extraordinary geographic dislocation. And the difficulty is compounded by what some have thought a misreading on Virgil's part. The suicide leap is another passage fashioned from two different "selections" from Theocritus. One is from *Idyll* I.134: "Let all things become confounded" (*enalla*)—not, as Virgil seems to have read, "Let all things become mid-sea" (*enalia*). The other is from *Idyll* III.25: "Into these waves shall I leap." Some critics have suggested that the goatherd's words are hallucinatory, that "the familiar bucolic landscape is engulfed in a cataclysmic vision"[8] that is only a vision, brought on by the mingling in the goatherd's imagination, just before he decides to die, of

> Orpheus in silvis, inter delphinas Arion

Orpheus in the woods, Arion among the dolphins.

The poor man, in other words, only imagines mid-sea where all is actually woods, and he falls to his death on the timbered mountain spot where he sang his song, utterly mad. If this reading is right, then perhaps Mount Maenalus did hear the goatherd's song. It is a mountain of madness, as its name indicates. Perhaps it answered the goatherd's prayer by making him mad.

Eclogue 8 goes on to an even more hallucinatory, if less memorable song. It is Virgil's full-scale version of the Theocritan poem he has already selected from—the song of the enchantress attempting to win her lover back (*Idyll* II). Virgil handily turns what was originally a mime to a pastoral poem by changing the lover's name from Delphis to Daphnis, by muting the more horrific and superstitious details, and by emphasizing the opposition between the imagined landscape, where the woman sings, and the city, where Daphnis is lingering. He also leaves it to us to determine whether there is but one enchantress, Amaryllis, talking to herself, or two—an anonymous woman conducting the ritual, and Amaryllis assisting her. Theocritus plainly has two women, speaker and servant, in his idyll, and his poem was often called, from its two women, *Pharmaceutriae*—the enchantresses. That, of course, is no guarantee that there are two women involved in Virgil's version. But I've chosen to think that there are two, and thus to keep the enchantress who sings this song as anonymous as the goatherd who sings of the apple orchard in the first half of the poem. Amaryllis I then take to be present at the incantation somewhat as Dido is in *Aeneid* IV, as a woman so desperately in love she employs a witch to win her lover back. (I also choose to read her references to Daphnis as *coniunx* in the Arcadian sense of that word, as "mate" or "lover". She only imagines Daphnis as "husband." Dido, too, imagined that of Aeneas.)

So, to a repeated refrain, various objects are dropped into a fire. In Theocritus' version, the incantation seems not to work. In Virgil's, to all appearances, it does. The fire dies out. The enchantress tells Amaryllis to take the ashes and cast them behind her into a running stream, without looking back. Amaryllis exclaims, "Look! I was slow to carry out the ashes, and they have burst spontaneously into flickering flame! They've lit up the whole altar! May it be a good omen!"

Has the spell worked? The enchantress changes her refrain from "Draw him, my spells, draw Daphnis from the city" to "Stop now, my spells, Daphnis comes from the city," but Amaryllis says only, "Something is happening, for the dog is barking in the doorway," and then, "Should we believe that something has happened, or do lovers only make their own dreams to suit themselves?"

Both the songs in *Eclogue* 8 are little dramas. Both singers attempt by incantation to win back a beloved. The man's song appears to end in a spectacular death in water (an archetypal feminine symbol) and the woman's to end in a spectacular burst of ashes into flame (an archetypal masculine symbol). The first appears to end with a song unanswered, the second with a song answered. But in fact both endings are ambiguous. Virgil leaves them open-ended.

To distance us from the stories, Virgil puts them in the mouths of herdsmen: the man's tale is told by Damon, the woman's by Alphesiboeus. They are sung just at dawn "when the dew on the tender grass is most delicious for the flocks," and they are so enchanting that "a heifer in amazement forgot about the grass, and wild lynxes listened stupefied." The lynxes called forth a comment from T.E. Page in his school edition. "Lynxes," he explained, "do not exist in Italy, but the whole scene is imaginary." Perhaps Page couldn't have known, in his century, that lynxes do range on Mount Maenalus, the Arcadian setting of the first half of the eclogue, and perhaps he couldn't have explained to his Victorian schoolboys that the lynxes are there to represent the wild irrational force of passionate love that animates both halves. But if the boys were young enough to remember their nursery days they would have understood intuitively why the lynxes were appropriate. A fairy-tale sensibility is sometimes needed to appreciate what Virgil is doing.

Then each song is set within a further frame. The "goatherd's song sung by Damon" is recounted by Virgil himself, and the "enchantress' song sung by Alphesiboeus" is recounted by the Muses. Virgil asks them to take over from him and sing the second song, explaining *non omnia possumus omnes*: "We can't all of us do everything." Does he sing only the first song because he finds its pessimism congenial? Or is it that he has a sense of his own limitations and those of the pastoral genre? (The second song is, after all, fashioned not from a pastoral poem but from a mime.) To move from the man's tormented realization of the destructive power of love to the woman's invocation of that destructive force may be more than he can, in his pastoral guise, command. He clearly wants to use the woman's song to give, in *Eclogue* 8, a complete picture of human nature. But he is only a man, and so perhaps he feels he knows only half of the human heart. *non omnia possumus omnes*. Let the Muses help him.

Finally, as we withdraw still further from the two incantatory poems, past the tormented man and woman, past the two herdsmen who sing of them, past Virgil and the Muses who recount them, we come to the outer world of politics and poetry, to the Roman commander who is, in the contemporary present, sailing along the coast of Illyria (Octavian, as recent scholarship contends[9]), and Virgil wonders if he will ever be able to sing to the world the epic or the drama of this man's deeds. Until the time that he can, he asks this man of beginnings and endings to accept the eclogue begun under his encouragement; let the pastoral ivy twine with the victorious leader's laurel. Virgil knows that the pastoral is only a preparatory stage for greater things, that something more portentous lies ahead for him. Meanwhile, exploring the pastoral nature of love, objectifying it in symbolic figures, distancing it, he is not happy with what he finds. Love, the elemental passion, is destructive. To feel it is to know the guilt humanity first felt when it became aware of itself and its potential for evil.

In his examination of love Virgil sets the tone for the whole pastoral tradition to follow. "The pastoral world," writes Peter Marinelli, "is the place where one learns that one is not passionless, that to assume that one is is to assume an innocence about human nature that is not in accord with reality. We are all given a capacity for love which is the common bond of humankind, but that love must be ordered and directed."[10] That, I think, is what Virgil intends in all the bantering bisexual activity in the *Eclogues;* he wants to represent love as a joyous force that animates all of nature, that must be acknowledged and welcomed, freely given and taken, never indulged or exploited. But he finds that, when love is isolated and intensified, as it is with some of the unfortunates on his landscape, it becomes, to quote again from A.J. Boyle, "turbulent, disorienting, uncontrollable and manic . . . a 'derangement' (*dementia,* E.2.69; E.6.47), 'frenzy' (*furor,* E.10.38, 60), 'madness' (*insanis,* E.10.22), which has no limit (E.2.68, E.10.28), seizes (E.2.69; E.6.47), burns (E.2.68; E.8.83), deceives (E.8.18; 91), distresses (E.2.58; E.6.47, 52; E.10.6), conquers (E.10.69), and is 'unworthy' (*indigno,* E.8.18; E.10.10)."[11] Romanticism at its extreme, in *Tristan und Isolde,* did not put it any more strongly.

With characteristic ambiguity, Virgil expresses the ambivalent potential of love when the man who had been the boy beneath the apple boughs leaps (or imagines he leaps) to his death. The poor man exclaims, "Let her have this last offering from me as I die":

extremum hoc munus morientis habeto.

The words seem rueful, even hateful, as if the man were offering his death as a wedding gift to the girl who left him for another. But the final *habeto* need not be a third person imperative addressed to the girl at all. It could be a second person imperative addressed to the chaotic world the unfortunate man is leaving. The words could be, not hateful, but hopeful: "O world, take this death as a final offering from me as I die." It is possible that the loveless suicide thinks that by his death he can restore to the world the innocence it once had for him. His *extremum munus* could then be the ideal of love as Virgil wants to see it—love generously given, directed outwards in hope rather than turned inwards in hate. That kind of love, given and received as the truly creative force it is, *could* transform the world.

But, our nature being flawed, it does not happen that way. And Virgil asks the Muses to sing the rest of *Eclogue* 8, his examination of human passion, for him. There is a *malus error,* a destructiveness in human nature, a perversion of love, that he did not want to sing of alone.

VIII

The City: Eclogues 1 and 9

No landscape is seen entirely, or in true perspective,
unless there is a city over the hill, glimpsed or at least sensed. John
Keats, contemplating a pastoral scene on his Grecian urn, wonders

> What little town by river or sea shore,
>   Or mountain-built with peaceful citadel,
>   Is emptied of this folk, this pious morn?

The pastoral is unthinkable without the city, be it Toronto or
Alexandria or Rome, that necessitates it. The pastoral, it might be
said, only exists because the city is there.

Critics of the pastoral often see it as an escape from the city, a
flight from the intolerable complexities of urban life to the
imagined simplicity of rustic existence such as, they insist, is
nowhere to be found in reality. That criticism may apply to some
later examples of the pastoral genre, but it is not true of Virgil. For
him the pastoral represents not escape but re-assessment, even
protest. In *Eclogues* 1 and 9 he makes a poet's grieving protest
against war, against the neglect of the land, against outrages
perpetrated on the innocent, against a way of living that has no
intuitive connection with nature and so can find no room for art.

All of these evils, myth ever since Hesiod tells us, come from
the city. Protected by its walls, subduing surrounding nature to its
will, it is one of the punishments visited on us by original sin, a
condition forced on the human race after the expulsion from
paradise.

The pastoral does not condemn the city as quickly as do the
myths. Though Virgil adopts Hesiodic language when it is

70

appropriate—as when the ages of man run back to their pristine gold in *Eclogue* 4, and the impulse towards city-building, along with warfare and navigation, appear to be traces left by some original sin *(priscae vestigia fraudis)*—he is generally of two minds about the city. It is an ambivalent place.

Viewed from Arcadia, Rome is specifically different from the little communities—cottages grouped around a market—that dot the pastoral landscape. You cannot take a Mariposa or a Mantua, multiply it over and over, and make a Toronto or a Rome. Any shepherd who makes his way to the city will come to know this, as Tityrus does in *Eclogue* 1:

> urbem, quam dicunt Romam, Meliboee, putavi
> stultus ego huic nostrae similem, quo saepe solemus
> pastores ovium teneros depellere fetus.
> sic canibus catulos similis, sic matribus haedos
> noram, sic parvis componere magna solebam.
> verum haec tantum alias inter caput extulit urbes
> quantum lenta solent inter viburna cupressi.
>
> (1.19–25)

The city that they call Rome I once foolishly thought,
Meliboeus, was like this place of ours, where we shepherds
Often and always drive down the tender young of our sheep.
That's all I knew—puppies were like mother dogs,
Kids like mother goats. That's all I knew—
How to measure big things by little things.
But *this* city lifts her head as high among others
As the cypress does among the bending undergrowth.

In *Eclogue* 1 Tityrus goes to this unArcadian Rome to buy his freedom *(libertas)*. Overawed, he sees a young man there who gives him, not his freedom—we never hear any more about that— but a mandate, along with other shepherds like him:

> pascite ut ante boves, pueri; summittite tauros
>
> Pasture your cattle as before, my children, tame your bulls.

Tityrus then returns to his country home to enjoy the peace *(otium)* he knew before. We inferred from this earlier that Virgil actually made a trip to Rome to see Octavian on behalf of the Mantuans, and an exemption (which we know is fact) was given the farmers (hence the plural *pueri* here) in the three-mile zone around Mantua. We may also infer that Virgil found, in the encounter in the city with Octavian, a patron who promised to protect him for the rest of his days, along with other promising young men of letters (hence the plural *pueri* here), in return for poetry in support of what was to become the Augustan peace.

But the overtones in the passage are difficult to sort out. Freedom and peace, *libertas* and *otium,* were political catch-words through the years in which the *Eclogues* were written. Julius Caesar used *libertas* as a slogan to justify his march on Rome. We have a fragment from Catullus (51a) and, later, an ode from Horace (2.16), and especially a passage in Cicero (*Philippics* 2.113) to indicate that the word *otium* was very much in the air, that it could be used by politicians to suit their own ends, that it sometimes meant, not peace, but subservience. Virgil found in the city a powerful ally who could protect him, by force if necessary, if he fulfilled his mandate: so Virgil-Tityrus pipes under a beechtree's *tegmen*—the word suggests a military shield. This is only a kind of *otium*: Virgil to the end of his days wrote what some have called propaganda, and he had doubts about the *libertas* he proclaimed.

The other rustic in *Eclogue* 1, Meliboeus, has met the city in another guise. He has been dispossessed of and evicted from his farm by a soldier who is *impius* and *barbarus*. "This is what civil war has led to!" he says. The city can send its citizens out to disrupt and destroy its own. If *Eclogue* 1 is like a Grecian urn, it is an urn to tease us out of thought. At first we see only two rustic figures in dialogue, one piping under a tree, the other herding his flocks. But as we look more closely, we notice that the one is happy and at peace, the other near to despair. Then, as we turn the urn from one side to the other, we see a benevolent youth standing behind the happy rustic, blessing him, while a barbarous soldier stands behind the despairing rustic, threatening him. Finally, on the reverse side of the urn, we see the city: ambivalent Rome has sent the godlike youth out in one direction, the godless soldier in the other. On the one hand, the happy piping rustic and the noble young man protecting him represent, we think, Virgil and Octavian. On the other—given the empathy Virgil always felt for the victimized, and the ruthlessness Octavian sometimes showed towards his victims—the dispossessed rustic and the barbarous soldier threatening him are, we think, Virgil and Octavian too. *Eclogue* 1 depicts the ambivalent relationship, not just between country and city, but between poet and patron.

The first eclogue has sometimes been accused, by those insensitive to the uses of poetry, of trivializing suffering. Such a reading is possible only if the reader identifies Virgil exclusively with the sheltered Tityrus. But in the desperate situation in Mantua in 42 B.C. Virgil could not but have sympathized as well with those Meliboeus represents. His nature was compassionate ("Why do the innocent suffer?" is one of the great Virgilian questions), and the antithetic cast of his mind would have impelled him to consider both sides of the question.

Often the two sides of a question are irreconcilable. We are not far into the poem before we realize that there is a psychological as well as a spatial distance between the two rustics. Tityrus speaks to Meliboeus, but never answers his questions directly. When he dreams on about never being able to forget the godlike youth, he even uses images that can only hurt the exiled Meliboeus: "Sooner will exiles cross on the way, each to the other's territory . . . than that young man's face will ever fade from my memory." It is as if Tityrus, on our imaginary urn, were facing away from Meliboeus, facing the youth who has given him his shelter and mandate to sing, while Meliboeus gazes sorrowfully but not enviously (*non invideo,* line 11) on Tityrus and describes, in memorable terms, the pastoral future he can never have. This first eclogue is like so many of the paintings of Renoir, in which each figure looks intently at another, and no one receives an answering glance. Each man is an island.

Virgil cannot reconcile the two conflicting feelings he has within himself. Only at the close of the eclogue does Tityrus think of sharing his plenty, and then his word *poteras* ("you *could have* rested this night here with me") tells us it is too late. The shadows are coming on. Shadows close in at the end of fully half of the eclogues, and they are almost always disquieting, blurring the outlines of the little pictures. At the close of *Eclogue* 1, we glimpse a most ambivalent scene through the lengthening shadows:

et iam summa procul villarum culmina fumant

away in the distance the smoke is already rising from the roofs of
farm houses.

What Tityrus sees as peacefully smoking chimneys (Rome has
saved the farms) Meliboeus might see as houses set on fire (Rome
has destroyed the farms).[1] Arcadia cannot ignore the ambivalent
city over the hill, whatever it is called. (For the Arcadia of history,
we think grimly, the city over the hill was Sparta.)

E.R. Curtius has observed that "from the first century of the
Empire to the time of Goethe, all study of Latin literature began
with the first eclogue. It is not too much to say that anyone
unfamiliar with that short poem lacks one key to the literary
tradition of Europe."[2] Certainly he lacks a key to reading five more
of the eclogues, in which two characters in dialogue represent the
poet himself seeking self-understanding. And as certainly he lacks
a key to Virgil's *Aeneid,* in which modern readers have heard two
voices—a public voice praising Augustus' accomplishment, and a
private voice wondering at the price paid for it in human suffering.[3]

Virgil treats the land confiscations and evictions in another
poem, the remarkable *Eclogue* 9, adapted from Theocritus's *Idyll*
VII. In the idyll, Theocritus himself, in the person of one
Simichidas, is making his way at high noon to a harvest festival.
Just before he sees a tomb on the landscape, he meets a mysterious
goatherd named Lycidas ("wolf son") who, after exchanging songs,
gives him his staff. Lycidas is, in some symbolic way, the power
that gives Theocritus his mandate to sing. The poet then proceeds
to the harvest feast, and we read one of the most remarkable
descriptions of bounteous nature in all of literature.

Virgil deepens and darkens this in *Eclogue* 9. He begins with
a brief but unmistakable quotation from Theocritus' poem: "Where
are your footsteps bent, Moeris?" (cf. *Idyll* VII.21). This time, the
mysterious Lycidas, on what may be thought his return journey
from the one he took in Theocritus, meets old Moeris. He meets, if
we read the name "Moeris" rightly, one "half" of Virgil—perhaps
his intuitive side, for we know, from *Eclogue* 8, that Moeris has
some contact with the world beyond. But now Moeris has been
expelled from his farm, and is driving his goats to their new master
(who has taken possession of the farm but chosen to live in the
city). Moeris had hoped to be exempted through the songs of—

Virgil may be meant here, too—Menalcas. But, Moeris continues, when he and Menalcas went together to make their representations to the soldiers in the city, their songs had as little effect in Mars' camp as prophetic doves have before the eagles of the Roman legions. In fact, they were lucky to have escaped with their lives. A raven from a hollow oak warned Moeris just in time.

Lycidas and Moeris continue on their journey, half remembering fragments of Menalcas' songs—two of them pastoral, two political, all of them very much in the style of Virgil. Moeris tells us that, from a strange encounter with wolves, he has lost his voice and forgotten all the songs he knew. Now, in another encounter with a wolf-figure, Lycidas, he is beginning to find his voice again.

Then the wind stops, the sea is still, the threat of rain is in the air, the farm hands are bundling leaves before the winter, and the two travelers come on the tomb that marks the landscape. It is not a Greek tomb, as in Theocritus, but the last resting place of the founder of Mantua.[4] So, in Virgil country, at a moment when all the land is poised for a storm, the two travelers wonder whether they should pause. Moeris says they'd better press on. They'll sing their half-remembered Menalcas-songs better when they meet Menalcas himself. They move on, not—as in Theocritus—to a bounteous harvest festival, but to an uncertain future in the city.

How are we to read this second eclogue on the evictions? It has baffled many commentators, and this reader (who feels it is about more than the evictions) can only offer a tentative and, he hopes, not too fanciful interpretation.

The unhappy Mantuans had depended on Virgil to protect their properties. But Virgil the vocal public figure (Menalcas), aided by his intuition, his inner half (Moeris), was unsuccessful in his mission. Since then he has gone from the land. His inner self, frightened by the encounter with Rome, has lost its outer, public voice. Now Lycidas, who once confirmed Theocritus in his mandate to sing, meets that inner half of Virgil and accompanies him on his way back to his outer self, helping him remember, bit by bit, the old forgotten songs. But Menalcas is not to be found any more on the pastoral landscape, which is threatened by a storm, and Moeris knows he must not pause at the landscape's tomb. It is time for a new kind of song. *Eclogue* 9 seems thus initially written to be the last of the eclogues, a farewell to Arcadia.

Virgil-Moeris passes on to a new destination, the city. Virgil-Menalcas has a new commitment there, and is awaiting the arrival of his prophetic genius.

The two eclogues on the land confiscations share a line that undergoes, from passage to passage, some interesting changes. In *Eclogue* 1 the city over the hill speaks benevolently to Tityrus and his fellow shepherds:

> pascite ut ante boves, pueri; summittite tauros
> Pasture your cattle as before, my children, tame your bulls.

In the same poem, the city has spoken malevolently to the evicted Meliboeus, and he rings changes on the line, keeping the metrical composition and optimistic thought, but weighting the words with rue:

> insere nunc, Meliboee, piros, pone ordine vitis
> Graft your pear trees now, Meliboeus, order your vines.

It is the most poignant cry of pain in all of the *Eclogues*.

Then in *Eclogue* 9 yet another change is rung on the line, as the metrical composition shifts slightly. Lycidas reminds Moeris of the song his voice Menalcas once sang:

> insere, Daphni, piros: carpent tua poma nepotes
> Graft your pear trees, Daphnis: your offspring will pluck the
>   fruit.

The line comes from a hopeful song, but Moeris as he plods on to the city says sadly that he cannot remember it any more.

However we read *Eclogues* 1 and 9, our feeling for the city over the hill is ambivalent.

IX

The Golden Age: Eclogue 4

Arcadia is constantly threatened, from within by the force of elemental passion, from without by the threat of war. This must be: if it is to be the place where poetry happens, it must know suffering and stress. It cannot be what it is popularly said to be, a never-never land where youth lasts forever, where nature is abundant and endlessly provident, and where there is no evil. When we read Virgil's *Eclogues,* some of the shepherds are old and some are slaves; nature is sometimes cruel; evil, in one form or another, seems to be almost everywhere. Virgil's Arcadia is often a sad, always a vulnerable place. As in the pastoral expressions of Sannazaro, Poussin, and Mozart (who was very pastoral when he composed in G and A Major), there are in Virgil shadows, sadnesses, strange contrasts for those who care to look beneath the placid surfaces.

But with Virgil the pastoral also begins to express the hope that a time will come when nature *will* provide all man's needs, and evil not exist, and the world live in the innocence of childhood. Virgil is in fact the first poet to sing that the Golden Age of the dawn of creation will return.

The Golden Age was, of course, sung of centuries before Virgil. But it was put irrevocably in the past. In the midst of *The Works and Days,* his farmer's manual and calendar, Hesiod describes human history as a long process of degeneration. The successive ages of man are like a succession of increasingly debased metals; they run from gold to silver to bronze to iron. Conditions in Hesiod's iron age are all but intolerable, as he works a resistant soil and the land is unnaturally measured off, and there is nothing to look forward to but senility and death. But there was, he says, a time when

The immortal gods who dwell on Olympus made a golden race
of mortal men.
They lived at the time of Cronus, when he was king in heaven.
Like gods they lived, with no sorrow in their hearts,
Far from toil and sadness. Miserable old age touched them
not at all.
With hands and feet ever youthful they delighted in goodly
feasting.
When they died, it was as if they were overcome by sleep.
All manner of good things were theirs. The bounteous earth
Spontaneously bore fruit abundant and endless.
They lived on their lands peacefully, just as they pleased,
Rich in flocks, and friends of the blessed gods.

(109–120)

The pastoral worlds of Theocritus and Virgil are already close
to this primitive paradise, lands half-way between the lost Golden
Age and the two poets' own experience, blending features of each.
But only Virgil sings that a time will come when the long-
since-receded Golden Age will move forward again and enfold his
Arcadia completely, and even his Rome partially, in the innocence
that the human race once knew. It was a bold declaration, this pa-
lingenesis, this optimistic reversal of the whole pessimistic lost Golden
Age tradition from Hesiod to his own day. It is a reversal comparable
to Goethe saving his Faust after the Faust myth had developed for
centuries in the opposite direction. Virgil too dared to alter radically
a long established myth, and succeeded in altering it forever after.
The comparison with Goethe might be extended a bit further: Virgil
anticipated Goethe's saving women—Gretchen, the Mothers, the Virgin Mary—when he introduced into his cosmic, mythic reversal the
Muses, the Sibyl, chaste Diana, and especially the Virgin Astraea,
last of the immortals to leave the earth at the time of man's sin. The
Virgin, he proclaims, is coming back. And Diana, in her role as
goddess of childbirth, is asked to smile on a newborn boy, and he to
recognize his mother with a smile.

The eclogue that predicts the return of the Golden Age,
Eclogue 4, has literary echoes far beyond the Hesiodic. It is in part
an answer to a cry of despair at the end of the longest and most
famous poem of Catullus, poem 64, on the wedding of Peleus and

Thetis. There Catullus recounts how the gods of Olympus once blessed a hero's marriage with their presence, and the Fates, spinning, predicted greatness for the child to be born of the happy union. But with the birth of the child (Achilles) and the subsequent outbreak of the Trojan War, Catullus says, the gods withdrew from the earth, and the age of heroes began its long decline—till in his own day humanity has reached extremes of violence and depravity.

A few years after Catullus, the young Horace wrote, in a similarly symbolic vein in his sixteenth epode, that the race had degenerated so markedly that a good man must seek an escape; Horace exhorts his fellow Romans to sail with him in an imaginary flight across Ocean stream to the Isles of the Blessed, where the heroes of the past live peacefully with the aged god, Saturn, who once blessed men on earth.

Virgil, writing about the same time as Horace (it is difficult to say who is answering whom[1]), insists in *Eclogue* 4 that Saturn's realm need not be sought in some far-off land; it is on the point of returning, soon, to Italy. If he is not directly answering Horace, he is most certainly responding to Catullus, for in words and sounds that echo poem 64[2] he imagines the imminent return of the gods who Catullus said had fled the earth, and he provides a peace-bestowing child to reverse the direction begun by the birth of Catullus' war-bringing Achilles.

For his prophecies in *Eclogue* 4, Virgil reached far and wide, to sources which are to some extent mutually contradictory: Hesiod's Golden Age myth and his "ages of man;" the similar myth of metals in Plato's *Republic;* the Pythagorean and Stoic notion of the Magnus Annus, the "great year" of peace which would come when the planets were aligned in the same positions as on the day of creation; and an Etruscan prophecy preserved in the books of the Sibyl of Cumae, in which the world would endure for ten *saecula,* or periods of one hundred and ten years, the last of them a time of great happiness, presided over by Apollo.

Of these sources, it is the Sibyl who best accounts for *Eclogue* 4's "Messianic" quality. A Sibyl from Cumae had figured in the legends of early Rome, and books purporting to be her prophecies were carefully preserved on the Capitoline and consulted by decree of the senate throughout the Republican period. When these were destroyed in the fire of 83 B.C., efforts were made to collect prophetic writings from all parts of the Romanized world to replace them. Virgil may thus have read and used "Sibylline books" of Jewish origin, perhaps even the *Oracula Sibyllina* which we still have,[3] and which contain passages distinctly reminiscent of Isaiah. Eventually the Sibyl was to be immortalized as the guide of Virgil's hero Aeneas through the underworld of *Aeneid* 6 and, in *Aeneid* 3, as the prophetess who entrusted her utterances to leaves, caring not at all if the winds scattered and lost them forever.

The fourth *Eclogue* is so famous, and ultimately so essential to our purposes, that it seems best to quote it complete, with running comment. But first-time readers should be forewarned. It is couched in the vague language of prophecy. Charles Fantazzi puts it nicely: "Like the dispersed leaves of the Sibyl, Virgil's sibylline transport is dislocated and fragmentary."[4]

> Sicelides Musae, paulo maiora canamus!
> non omnis arbusta iuvant humilesque myricae;
> si canimus silvas, silvae sint consule dignae.

> Muses of Sicily, let us sing a somewhat more serious strain!
> Orchards and earth-bound tamarisks are not to everyone's taste.
> If sing of trees we must, let the trees be of consular rank.

So Virgil takes leave of the Sicilian themes of the preceding *Eclogues* 2 and 3, of the ordinary landscape with its tamarisks (pastoral symbols of the lowly), and addresses himself to higher subject matter (*silvae*, like the Greek *hyle*, may imply matter to be shaped[5]). This most ambitious of the eclogues must be worthy of a consul (Pollio, eventually named in line 12, was consul in 40 B.C.). The language here is alliterative, as prophetic language usually was, and Virgil spreads his first word, *Sicelides*, across his third line in a marvelous alliterative pattern:

> *si c*animus *sil*vas, *sil*vae *s*int *c*onsu*l*e *di*gnae.

> ultima Cumaei venit iam carminus aetas;
> magnus ab integro saeclorum nascitur ordo.
> iam redit et Virgo, redeunt Saturnia regna,
> iam nova progenies caelo demittitur alto.
> tu modo nascenti puero, quo ferrea primum

desinet ac toto surget gens aurea mundo,
casta fave Lucina: tuus iam regnat Apollo.

Now has come the final age that was sung of at Cumae.
The mighty march of the centuries begins anew.
Now the Virgin comes again, Saturn's kingdom comes again.
Now is a new race of men sent down from heaven on high.
And as the boy is born who will end at last
The iron age, and bring the world the age of gold,
Bless him, chaste Lucina. Your Apollo rules us now.

In these lines Virgil cites his three major sources of prophecy: the predictions of the Sibyl at Cumae, the Magnus Annus of Stoic thought, and the mythological traditions that Saturn once lived among men in Italy and that the virgin Astraea, goddess of justice, once left the world, last of all the gods to do so, when the human race learned to sin. The three sources, which Virgil does not attempt to fuse, converge as (to give an interpretation) the Virgin come back from heaven gives birth to a baby boy, and the course of human history reverts from base iron to pristine gold. The birth of a divine child is a motif found in many near-Eastern traditions, from Macrobius' reference to Alexandrian Aion, the Sun born in the winter solstice (*Saturnalia* 1.18.10) to Isaiah 7.14 ("Behold a Virgin shall conceive and bear a son, and shall call his name Immanuel [God-with-us]")—either or both of which Virgil could have consciously used. In the last line, Diana (called Lucina, "light-bearing," as she brings children to the light) is asked to favor the boy because his birth marks the astrological ascendance of her brother Apollo, the sun god. The seven lines set the numerical pattern for the poem, which may be divided into sections as follows: 3–7–7–28–7–7–4 (with the 3 lines at the start = 7).

teque adeo decus hoc aevi, te consule, inibit,
Pollio, et incipient magni procedere menses;
te duce, si qua manent sceleris vestigia nostri,
inrita perpetua solvent formidine terras.
ille deum vitam accipiet divisque videbit
permixtos heroas et ipse videbitur illis,
pacatumque reget patriis virtutibus orbem.

This glorious age will start with you, Pollio, you as consul.
The mighty months will start their onward movement.
With you as guide, the traces of our guilt that linger
Will be absolved, and earth set free at last from fear.
The child will live to be a god; he'll see the gods
And heroes all together, and be seen in turn by them.
He'll rule a world made peaceful by his father's goodness.

The return of the Golden Age will be a gradual process, only
beginning in the consulship of Pollio. But eventually it will bring
absolution from the traces of *scelus,* a word which can refer equally
to a mythic original sin or to the civil wars of Virgil's own century
(a double significance *scelus* also bears in Horace's *Epode* 7).
Similarly *patriis virtutibus* can refer equally to the father in such
passages as Isaiah 9.6–7 ("For unto us a child is born, unto us a son
is given: and the government shall be upon his shoulder: and his
name shall be called Wonderful, Counsellor, The mighty God, The
everlasting Father, The Prince of Peace.") and to the prospective
fathers Pollio, Antony, and Octavian at the Peace of Brundisium.

> at tibi prima, puer, nullo munuscula cultu
> errantis hederas passim cum baccare tellus
> mixtaque ridenti colocasia fundet acantho.
> ipsae lacte domum referent distenta capellae
> ubera, nec magnos metuent armenta leones;
> ipsa tibi blandos fundent cunabula flores.
> occidet et serpens, et fallax herba veneni
> occidet; Assyrium vulgo nascetur amomum.
> at simul heroum laudes et facta parentis
> iam legere et quae sit poteris cognoscere virtus,
> molli paulatim flavescet campus arista
> incultisque rubens pendebit sentibus uva
> et durae quercus sudabunt roscida mella.
> pauca tamen suberunt priscae vestigia fraudis,
> quae temptare Thetim ratibus, quae cingere muris
> oppida, quae iubeant telluri infindere sulcos.
> alter erit tum Tiphys et altera quae vehat Argo
> delectos heroas; erunt etiam altera bella
> atque iterum ad Troiam magnus mittetur Achilles.
> hinc, ubi iam firmata virum te fecerit aetas,
> cedet et ipse mari vector, nec nautica pinus

mutabit merces; omnis feret omnia tellus.
non rastros patietur humus, non vinea falcem;
robustus quoque iam tauris iuga solvet arator;
nec varios discet mentiri lana colores,
ipse sed in pratis aries iam suave rubenti
murice, iam croceo mutabit vellera luto;
sponte sua sandyx pascentis vestiet agnos.

But first, o child, the earth will pour forth for you everywhere,
With no cultivation, pretty little gifts—wand'ring ivy
With foxglove mixed, Egyptian bean with laughing acanthus.
Untended will the goats fare home, their udders taut
With milk, the herds will have no fear of lions' might.
Unprompted will your cradle pour forth delicate flowers.
The serpent will die. The deceiving poison-plant
Will die, Assyrian spikenard spring up everywhere.
Then, once you learn to read of heroes' praise, what father did,
What great men are, little by little then
The fields will gold with tender grain,
The ruddy grape will hang on briars wild,
The liquid honey ooze from hardy oaks.
Traces, few, will linger of our guilty past
To urge us brave the sea in ships, to gird
Our towns with walls, to furrow earth.
Another Tiphys then will sail, another Argo
Carry chosen men, and other oars there'll be,
Some great Achilles sent again to Troy.
But then, when passing years have made you hero-strong,
The sailor will himself forsake the sea, and pinewood ships
No longer ply their trade. Each land will bear each good,
The earth endure no mattock, the vine no pruning hook
The sturdy ploughman free his oxen from the yoke
And wool unlearn the lies of diverse hues:
The ram in the field will change his fleece himself
Now to saffron yellow, now to purple blushing-sweet.
Vermillion of its own will clothe the grazing lambs.

In this central passage, the "pretty little gifts" spontaneously
produced symbolize poetry (ivy), artistry (acanthus), protection
from evil (foxglove), the universalizing of the particular (plants
peculiar to Egypt and Assyria springing up all over the world). The

death of poisonous fauna and flora signify the end of nature's disharmony with man. The whole picture conforms generally with Golden Age descriptions from Hesiod onwards with, again, touches reminiscent of Isaiah 11.6 ("The calf and the young lion and the fatling together, and a little child shall lead them") and 11.8 ("The sucking child shall play on the hole of the asp"), and perhaps even of *Genesis* 3:15, on the woman's child and the serpent ("He shall bruise your head"). But of course heroes in many mythologies prove their manhood by slaying dragons. Virgil leaves everything open to the widest interpretation.

As the child reaches adolescence and goes "about his father's business" (a familiar strain in the monomyth of the hero), Virgil's description of the Golden Age also gathers force with motifs familiar to us from their later use by Ovid (*Metamorphoses* I) and from Isaiah 55.13 ("Instead of the thorn shall come up the fir tree, and instead of the brier shall come up the myrtle tree"). But a reader in 40 B.C. would know that world peace could not be expected immediately, with Caesar's assassins still unpunished, and with Antony and Octavian still jockeying for power. So, on the eclogue's upward movement from iron back to gold, the race must pass again through the old age of heroes—with the land-tilling, sea-trawling, and city-fortifying imposed in the age of Achilles and the earlier time when Tiphys piloted the Argo. (In Hesiod, the three activities are all punishments for original sin, and Virgil accordingly refers to them as caused by "traces of our guilty past". *Priscae vestigia fraudis* is a phrase even more suggestive of the sins of Prometheus and Lycaeus than the *sceleris vestigia nostri* earlier in the poem). Virgil's contemporaries could read in the passage, if they chose, the civil wars still to be fought.

Finally, by the time the child reaches manhood, the Golden Age will have dawned in all its fullness. There will be no more traces of the sinful past, no more citified artifice like garments dyed in purple and gold—though the "sheep of a different color" that will end such extravagances is itself something of an extravagance. Servius (*ad loc.*) and Macrobius (*Saturnalia* 3.7.2) tell us it is from Etruscan prophetic lore, and a symbol of happiness to the fullest; the reader may also think of Isaiah 40.11 ("He shall feed his flock like a shepherd").

'Talia saecla' suis dixerunt 'currite' fusis
concordes stabili fatorum numine Parcae.
adgredere o magnos (aderit iam tempus) honores,
cara deum suboles, magnum Iovis incrementum!
aspice convexo nutantem pondere mundum,
terrasque tractusque maris caelumque profundum;
aspice, venturo laetantur ut omnia saeclo!

Once the Parcae told their spindles, "Spin those ages on"
In concord with the fixed decree of Fate.
So, on to your great honors, child! The time is near,
Dear child of gods, great increment of Jove.
See how the vast round world bows down—
Lands and tracts of sea and depthless sky.
See how all creation joys in the times to come!

Here, with the only past tense used in the poem, we have an unquestionable reference to Catullus 64, the pessimistic poem Virgil is responding to. When Catullus' Fates predicted the birth of the boy Achilles, they sang the refrain:

Currite ducentes subtegmina, currite fusi.

Virgil echoes some of that line to mark the contrast between the age of war Achilles brought and the age of peace the divine child will bring. From this vantage point we can look back on the eclogue and see other contrasts: Catullus' gods leave the earth, Virgil's return; Catullus excludes from his wedding Diana and Apollo, Virgil invokes them; in Catullus sin leads to sin, in Virgil the traces of sin are gradually eliminated.

More than half of Virgil's lines are colored by Catullus;[6] this is best seen in Virgil's uncharacteristic use of a word-order favored by Catullus in poem 64, an order John Dryden coincidentally calls "Golden": "two substantives and two adjectives with a verb betwixt to keep the peace." The wonderful effect of the Golden Line is that, as with a fresco gradually coming clear as it dries, or as with the Golden Age gradually dawning, the line comes clear only as the eye moves across it: the descriptive details are presented first, in the two adjectives, then the verb activates the picture, and finally we see the nouns to which the details apply. Virgil's Golden Lines in *Eclogue* 4 are:

> ultima Cumaei venit iam carminis aetas
> ipsa tibi blandos fundent cunabula flores
> incultisque rubens pendebit sentibus uva,

though perhaps the most illustrative such line has an adverb for the second adjective:

> molli paulatim flavescet campus arista.

For the rest, Virgil's heavy word *incrementum* turns the dactylic verse solemnly spondaic for a moment, calls up more memories of Isaiah ("a child is born . . . and his name shall be called Wonderful, Counsellor, The mighty God"), and above all emphasizes the idea of gradual growth, even as Octavian was eventually to accept a name implying growth and fulfillment—Augustus. Finally, the word *nutantem* ("bowing" or perhaps "trembling") suggests that the birth of the child has the nature of an epiphany in Arcadia—the earth quakes with joy.

> o mihi tum longae maneat pars ultima vitae,
> spiritus et quantum sat erit tua dicere facta!
> non me carminibus vincet nec Thracius Orpheus,
> nec Linus, huic mater quamvis atque huic pater adsit,
> Orphei Calliopea, Lino formosus Apollo.
> Pan etiam, Arcadia mecum si iudice certet,
> Pan etiam Arcadia dicat se iudice victum.

Oh, may my life endure till I see this happen!
May I have spirit enough to sing of your exploits!
Then Orpheus of Thrace would not in song prove better,
Nor Linus—though the mother aid the one, and one the father,
Calliopea on Orpheus' side, on Linus' Apollo.
Should Pan himself, with Arcadia as judge, vie with me,
Then Pan himself, with Arcadia as judge, would say he'd been
    bested.

Here Virgil, confident that the birth of the child will give him inspiration enough, prays for a life sufficiently long to write the poem that will eventually be the *Aeneid*. His confidence becomes cheerfully blasphemous, in an Arcadian context, when he

challenges Pan himself. The ultimate importance of this section is
that Virgil sees in the transformation of the world a transformation
in himself as poet.

> incipe, parve puer, risu cognoscere matrem
> (matri longa decem tulerunt fastidia menses)
> incipe, parve puer: qui non risere parenti,
> nec deus hunc mensa, dea nec dignata cubili est.

Begin, little boy, to recognize your mother with a smile.
Ten months have brought your mother much weariness.
Begin, little boy. The boy who does not smile at his parents
No god will deign to board, no goddess deign to bed.

These four lines together with the initial three make up the desired
and prophetic number seven. What sounds like Christmas-card
sentiment in the first line reaches beyond the child-god of the
Christians; Fantazzi observes, "If the child is to attain divinity he
must give some sign of his heavenly calling. Pan had laughed at
birth, as had Zoroaster, a tradition from Iranian religion which may
well have been circulated by the Sibyl."[7] The line also evokes
Catullus, who hoped to see a smile from the boy to be born of the
union celebrated in his poem 61.

Virgil's last line, with its reference to bed and board among
the gods, is a deliberately optimistic thought to set beside the
pessimistic conclusion of Catullus 64, where men have forgotten
the gods and defiled the rites of hospitality and wedlock. The last
line could thus be thought a graceful tribute to Pollio (who knew
Catullus and very likely prized poem 64), or, by another token, to
Antony (whose chosen ancestor, Hercules, was admitted to
Jupiter's board and Hebe's bed), or to Octavian (the founder of
whose Julian line, Anchises, was admitted to Venus' bed).[8] To the
end, Virgil leaves every possibility open.

Finally, the word order of the last line, doubling in on itself,
continues the sound patterns in the previous section's *Pan etiam
Arcadia . . . si iudice / Pan etiam Arcadia . . . se iudice* and this
section's *incipe, parve puer . . . matrem / matri . . . incipe parve
puer*. The end of the poem is thus at once literate, playful,
ambivalent—and couched in the alliterative language of prophecy.

One last word on the identity of the child. In a historical perspective he might represent, not so much the son each of the three politicians was expecting, as the promise of the moment, 40 B.C., when the century of war seemed almost to be over, when world events were at a turning point, when a poet could entertain the hope that the men in power might come to terms and the race not destroy but perfect itself.

On a level personal to Virgil himself—and increasingly we feel that every symbol in the *Eclogues* reflects something of the imagining poet—the child might represent the promise Virgil hopes to fulfill as a poet. William Berg[9] has pointed out that almost all the shepherd poets in the *Eclogues* are called *pueri*; that the *puer* in *Eclogue* 4 is given a poet's insignia (ivy and foxglove); that the *puer*'s predicted career parallels the stages of Virgil's own growth from *Eclogues* (lines 18–25) to *Georgics* (28–30) to *Aeneid* (26–7 and 31–6); that *incipe*, the command twice given the boy, is used elsewhere only in the sense of "begin to sing." Further, the *heroum laudes* in line 26 sound like a Latinization of the *klea andrōn* recounted by the hero of the *Iliad* (9.524) and thus "once you learn to read of heroes' praise" can mean in effect "once you have read Homer and can adapt him to Latin in an epic poem of your own." The *quae sit poteris cognoscere virtus* in line 27 is a sentiment Virgil will put in the mouth of his hero Aeneas, who says to his young son as he kisses him through his helmet, "Learn from me what it is to be a man and to suffer." The child, then, could well be the poetry that Virgil feels gestating within him.

The "Messianic Eclogue" is a poem unparalleled among the short poems in Latin for imagination and complexity, and unique among the eclogues for the mounting sense of excitement before its quiet, light-hearted, unsentimental close (with a last line as subtly open to interpretation as any of the more highly charged lines that precede it). By all odds this poem should mark a transition in the collection of eclogues, or come last, or occupy a central place of honor. Strangely, it does none of these things. The eclogue that is centrally placed (numerically in the exact center between poems 1 and 9) is about death, not birth. We turn now to *Eclogue* 5.

X

Death: Eclogue 5

Virgil did not write the haunting, elusive line *"Et in Arcadia ego,"* though many people suppose that it is to be found somewhere in the *Eclogues*. Their instinct is sound enough. *"Et in Arcadia ego"* is a phrase that may be thought to capture the essential spirit of Virgil's pastorals, provided it be properly understood. For perhaps two centuries it was read to mean "I was once in Arcadia, too." The speaker—Goethe, for example, remembering his *Italienische Reise*—looks back at a time when he was young and happy in a beautiful landscape. This is a mis-reading.

When we first meet the phrase, in a painting done in about 1621 by Guercino (Giovanni Francesco Barbieri), it is spoken by Death. And it has not a past but a present force. In Guercino's painting, now in the Galleria Corsini in Rome, two wandering shepherds come upon a tomb surmounted by a skull. Inscribed on the tomb are the words the skull, if it could speak, would say: *"Et in Arcadia ego"*—"I too am in Arcadia" or perhaps, *"Even* in Arcadia I am present."* This, we now think, is the correct meaning, the original sense of the phrase.[1] It is meant to convey not blissful nostalgia but a sense of the immediacy of death. Even in the enclosure where all is supposedly timeless happiness, death is present.

As Guercino's theme continued in the works of other painters, and eventually passed into the literatures of Europe, the phrase was not only mis-interpreted but re-arranged (*et ego in Arcadia*) and equipped with past-tense verbs (*fui, vixi*) which perpetuated the mis-interpretation. It is now almost impossible to say when and with whom the phrase originated. It seems not to be Guercino's

89

own but to have been suggested, along with the idea of Death speaking, to Guercino by the humanist Giulio Rospigliosi, later Pope Clement IX. (The matter is further complicated by the fact that for many years Guercino's painting, and the phrase it interpreted, were wrongly ascribed to Bartolommeo Schidone.)

In any case, the words have caught and conveyed something of the melancholy sense of mortality peculiar to Virgil. Theocritus' wandering figure for himself (Simichidas meeting Lycidas in *Idyll* VII) never reaches a vantage point where he can view the tomb on the landscape, but Virgil's (Moeris meeting Lycidas in *Eclogue* 9) can see a tomb in the distance, just coming into view. And in *Eclogue* 5 we have the classic anticipation of *"Et in Arcadia ego"*: Virgil has two herdsmen move from a spot "where the elms and the hazels mingle" to a cave "which the wild woodland vine dapples here and there with grape clusters," from a place which will allow only *incertas umbras,* intermittent darkness, to a place where, presumably, no sunlight penetrates—the cave, if you will, of the unconscious, hung about with the clusters of the irrational and intuitive Dionysus. There, in what may be thought the very center[2] of the *Eclogues,* young Mopsus sings to older Menalcas a song on the essential Arcadian theme and the essential Arcadian hero: he sings of the death of Daphnis.

> Extinctum Nymphae crudeli funere Daphnin
> flebant (vos coryli testes et flumina Nymphis)
> cum complexa sui corpus miserabile nati
> atque deos atque astra vocat crudelia mater.
> non ulli pastos illis egere diebus
> frigida, Daphni, boves ad flumina, nulla neque amnem
> libavit quadripes nec graminis attigit herbam.
> Daphni, tuum Poenos etiam ingemuisse leones
> interitum montesque feri silvaeque loquuntur.

The nymphs wept for Daphnis when he died his cruel death
(You hazels and rivers are witness for them),
When his mother held her son's poor body in her arms
And called the gods and stars of heaven cruel.
O Daphnis! No one in those days could drive his bulls
From pasture to cool stream, and no four-footed one
In those days lapped the river, grazed the grass.

O Daphnis! Punic lions even wailed your death!
(Our mountain wilds and forests tell us so.)

    Daphnis et Armenias curru subiungere tigris
    instituit, Daphnis thiasos inducere Bacchi
    et foliis lentas intexere mollibus hastas.
    vitis ut arboribus decori est, ut vitibus uvae,
    ut gregibus tauri, segetes ut pinguibus arvis,
    tu decus omne tuis. postquam te fata tulerunt,
    ipsa Pales agros atque ipse reliquit Apollo.
    grandia saepe quibus mandavimus hordea sulcis,
    infelix lolium et steriles nascuntur avenae;
    pro molli viola, pro purpureo narcisso
    carduus et spinis surgit paliurus acutis.

It was Daphnis taught us to yoke Armenian tigers to chariot,
It was Daphnis taught us to lead Bacchic troops in procession,
And to soften our spears with gentle leaves.
As the vine graces the tree and the grape the vine,
As the bull graces the herd and the crop the fertile field,
So you were all grace to your people. When Fate bore you off,
Pales herself, Apollo himself left the land.
From furrows where full oft we sowed big barley gains,
Darnel weeds and barren straw have sprung.
Where once grew gentle violet, where once narcissus bright,
The thistle and the spiky thorn arise.

    spargite humum foliis, inducite fontibus umbras,
    pastores (mandat fieri sibi talia Daphnis),
    et tumulum facite, et tumulo superaddite carmen:
    'Daphnis ego in silvis, hinc usque ad sidera notus,
    formosi pecoris custos, formosior ipse.'

Strew earth with leaves, ye shepherds, shade the springs!
Daphnis commands these rites be done for him.
Build him a tomb, and on it put a song:
"Daphnis was I in the forest, known from here to the sky.
Mine was a handsome flock, handsomer still was I."

This song, sung in a cave replete with Bacchic symbols, is an attempt to intuit anew what the Daphnis myth might mean. It is remarkably different from Theocritus' first *Idyll*,[3] where Daphnis is dying, and Aphrodite comes to triumph over him, and he calls on nature to mark his death by being fruitful in impossible ways, with violets on thorn bushes, narcissus on junipers, pears on pine tees. Here, Daphnis is not dying but already dead; the goddess who appears is not his enemy Venus but his weeping mother; it is not impossible fruition but a terrible blight that has come on the land, a blight felt even across the Sicilian sea in Punic Africa by the lions on that landscape. The song is, in short, something of a reversal of Theocritus.

It reverses as well the promise of the "Messianic Eclogue" placed just before it in the collection. There Apollo and the Virgin return to earth, here Apollo and the goddess Pales withdraw; there the land burgeons, here it withers; there the divine child is invited to proceed to the heights of achievement, here the shepherds are carving the epitaph for a tomb; there the new-born boy smiles at his mother, here the son is dead and the mother weeps.

Then, in a song of exactly equal length, Menalcas replies to Mopsus that all is not over:

> Candidus insuetum miratur limen Olympi
> sub pedibusque videt nubes et sidera Daphnis.
> ergo alacris silvas et cetera rura voluptas
> Panaque pastoresque tenet Dryadesque puellas.
> nec lupus insidias pecori, nec retia cervis
> ulla dolum meditantur: amat bonus otia Daphnis.
> ipsi laetitia voces ad sidera iactant
> intonsi montes; ipsae iam carmina rupes,
> ipsa sonant arbusta: 'deus, deus ille, Menalca!'

Vested in white Daphnis stands, all amazed, at the gate of
    Olympus.
He sees the clouds, the stars beneath his feet.
And that is why heart-piercing joy floods through the woods,
Through all the land, through Pan, the shepherds and dryad
    maids.
The wolf contrives no ambush for the flock, the nets no guile
For deer. Our goodly Daphnis loves the ways of peace.
For very happiness the uncropped mountains cast their cry
To the stars, the very rocks ring out their song,
The very trees resound, "He is a god, a god, Menalcas!"

sis bonus o felixque tuis! en quattuor aras:
ecce duas tibi, Daphni, duas altaria Phoebo.
pocula bina novo spumantia lacte quotannis
craterasque duo statuam tibi pinguis olivi,
et multo in primis hilarans convivia Baccho
(ante focum, si frigus erit; si messis, in umbra)
vina novum fundam calathis Ariusia nectar.
cantabunt mihi Damoetas et Lyctius Aegon;
saltantis Satyros imitabitur Alphesiboeus.
haec tibi semper erunt, et cum solemnia vota
reddemus Nymphis, et cum lustrabimus agros.

O Daphnis, be gracious and kind to your people. Look, here are
　　four altars,
See, two for you and two for Apollo. His are for high feasts,
Yours are for two cups afoam with fresh milk—every year
Those I'll offer, and two jars awash with olive oil,
And more than that, while feasting merrily, with wine flowing
　　free
(Before the fire, if it's cold, if it's harvest time, in the shade),
I'll pour you fresh nectar, Ariusian vintage, from my flasks.
Damoetas will sing for me, and Aegon from Crete, and
Alphesiboeus will leap high to please us, mimicking satyrs.
These rituals will be yours, forever, both when we render
Our solemn vows to the nymphs and when we purify the land.

dum iuga montis aper, fluvios dum piscis amabit,
dumque thymo pascentur apes, dum rore cicadae,
semper honos nomenque tuum laudesque manebunt.
ut Baccho Cererique, tibi sic vota quotannis
agricolae facient: damnabis tu quoque votis.

So long as the boar loves the hilltop, the fish the stream,
So long as bees feed on thyme, and crickets dew,
That long will your fame and your name and your praises remain.
Just as long as the countryfolk pay their vows to Bacchus and
　　Ceres,
So long will they pay them to you. And you will bind them and
　　loose them.

Here, hard on the heels of Mopsus' Dionysian reversal of the
"Messianic Eclogue," we have Menalcas' Apollonian restatement

of it. The optimistic future tenses of that poem and the pessimistic
past tenses of Mopsus' song in this poem merge in a radiant
present, as Daphnis in the world above sends blessings, as the
shepherds below promise sacrifices to their new god, as the land is
cleansed and nature returns to its normal pattern. Again, there are
suggestions of Isaiah (11.6: "The wolf also shall dwell with the
lamb," and 55.12: "The mountains and the hills shall break forth
before you into singing, and all the trees of the field shall clap their
hands"). But, we remind ourselves again as well, there are many
mythic figures that also fit the pattern, most notably the vegetation
gods Tammuz, Linus, Adonis, and Attis.[4] And anyone reading the
passage in the late 40s B.C. would certainly think of Julius Caesar
(murdered in 44, deified in 42) and associate the Julian family's
Venus with the sorrowing mother, Caesar's patronage of Carthage
with the Punic lions, his plan to restore the war-torn Italian
countryside with the flowering spear, his monument in the forum
with the shepherd's tomb and inscription, the star that appeared at
his funeral with the ascent of Daphnis above the stars.[5] As with the
"Messianic Eclogue," so here Virgil provides clues to allow a
contemporary interpretation, and leaves the matter open.

The literary cross-references we expect in Virgil (overwhelm-
ingly so in the *Aeneid*) are very much here. Virgil's *deus, deus ille,
Menalca* echoes Lucretius on his godlike master Epicurus (5.8:
deus ille fuit, deus, inclute Memmi), and when at the end of the
songs his two singers exchange pipe and staff we think of the end
of Theocritus' *Idyll* VII, where one of the singers represents the
poet himself. Here, Virgil identifies one of his two singers,
Menalcas, as himself when he has him claim, at the close, to have
written "Formosum Corydon ardebat Alexin" (*Eclogue* 2) and
"Quoium pecus? an Meliboei?" (*Eclogue* 3).

An opera-goer reading *Eclogue* 5 will think of other
resonances still. He will think at least twice of Wagner. He will
think, first, of the third act of *Die Meistersinger*. Virgil's young
singer and older master come together to compose a song, and
older Menalcas tactfully encourages the talented but touchy young
Mopsus to sing something different from Apollo's and Amyntas'
songs, and the boy sings something the like of which the man has
never heard. It is as if Wagner's older, wiser Hans Sachs and proud
young Walther von Stolzing were at the mouth of Virgil's cave,

even to the detail of Mopsus' writing his song down (unheard of in the pastoral tradition) and the final exchange of gifts, like the exchange of the girl and the laurel at the end of Wagner's opera. And as Walther and Sachs are clearly two reconciling aspects of Wagner's personality so, it has occurred to commentators,[6] Mopsus and Menalcas may represent the young and the maturing Virgil, the pessimist and the potential optimist.

Even more, Wagner (no admirer of Virgil but like Virgil one of our great intuitors) seems, in his tragic operas and especially in *Tristan und Isolde,* to have found and explored the idea of death suggested in Daphnis' myths. Like Theocritus' Daphnis, Wagner's heroes and heroines *will* their deaths. Most of them do not die of any natural causes. Those who do so die of wounds or suicides that are also symbols of transcendence. Increasingly in the later works, they die because they see passion as a destructive force that must be renounced. Tristan and Isolde die as a consequence of an unfulfilled erotic passion that, like the *furor* and the *dementia* of the *Eclogues,* seizes, burns, deceives, and rages uncontrolled until stilled by death.[7] The fruitfulness of these willed deaths in Wagner is expressed finally in external symbols—the calm sea for Senta and the Dutchman, the evening star for Elisabeth and the greening papal scepter for Tannhäuser, the restored child-ruler for Elsa, the purification of the world for Brünnhilde and Siegfried, the restoration of the Holy Grail for Kundry.

It may be objected that Virgil's Daphnis is not even Theocritus' dying hero, let alone Wagner's: Virgil never says that his Daphnis willed to die at all. He couldn't keep that idea in *Eclogue* 5 and still suggest the parallel with the death of Julius Caesar. But he does develop the idea in *Eclogue* 10 where, as we shall see in the next chapter, his friend Gallus will unexpectedly act out the role of the Theocritan Daphnis, willing his own death—and the fruitfulness of that death will be expressed, most memorably, in an external symbol.

Eclogue 5 rightly comes at the center of the collection: death, as the famous phrase has it, is in Arcadia, and central to any notion of the pastoral. But death is imminent at the end of the *Eclogues* as well. We turn now to the symbolic love-death, not of Daphnis, but of the flesh-and-blood Roman astonishingly cast in the role of Daphnis—Virgil's beloved Gallus.

XI

Leaving Arcadia: Eclogue 10

Several times in the *Eclogues* Virgil shows that he is aware of great events outside his Arcadia, and the thought occurs to him that a serious poet ought to be in the thick of those events, pondering, interpreting, perhaps even celebrating them. But he knows he is not yet ready. He does shift to higher styles in *Eclogues* 4 (prophecy), 6 (Alexandrian epyllion), and 8 (balancing and contrasting Theocritean subjects), and significantly in each case he addresses an important public figure—Pollio, Varus, Octavian—with a word about his pastoral art being inadequate even to those efforts. It was inevitable that a poet of his promise would someday leave Arcadia for the larger world. *Eclogue* 9, with Lycidas and Moeris journeying to the city, seems to have been written as his farewell to the pastoral world. Eventually, though, Virgil added a more formal farewell, *Eclogue* 10.

Virgil's time in Arcadia was, as it turned out, a preparation for the more ambitious and politically committed *Georgics* and the ultimate meditation on, and to some extent celebration of, empire—the epic *Aeneid*. The pastoral genre has often served as an initial stage in the shaping of a poet—Politian, Sannazaro, Tasso, Spenser, Milton, and Pope were all Arcadians before they moved on to larger concerns. Fledgling heroes too—the young Siegfried and Arthur and Luke Skywalker—undergo a period of special education in the forest before they embark on their adventures. Even that mature hero Aeneas travels, in *Aeneid* 8, up the Tiber to a land of Arcadians before he commits himself to his wars in Italy.

The trip to Arcadia makes the poet or the hero aware of himself, for everything he sees in Arcadia's closed space is a metaphor for himself, and himself in a postlapsarian state in which

96

he is conscious of both the good and the evil that lie in his heart. The experience returns the hero, or the poet, to his mission in the wider world with a realistic view of what he is, what the future may hold, and how he is to accomplish it. T.H. White's King Arthur finds from living among the fishes, badgers, and birds the inspiration for his Camelot, and Virgil's Aeneas finds in his up-Tiber Arcadia the site where his Rome will eventually be built. Something similar can be said for the various characters who return from their temporary retreats in Shakespeare's *As You Like It, A Midsummer Night's Dream,* and *The Tempest.*

But Virgil knows that too long a stay in Arcadia can turn a poet excessively inward. In the end he says

> surgamus: solet esse gravis cantantibus umbra,
> iuniperi gravis umbra; nocent et frugibus umbrae.
> ite domum saturae, venit Hesperus, ite capellae.

Let us arise. The shade is bad for singers.
The shade of the juniper is bad; shadows can harm the fruits, too.
Fare home, my kids. You've fed your full. The evening comes
    on. Fare home.

This last farewell, *Eclogue* 10, the most baffling of them all, re-introduces Gallus, the soldier captured by love, and puts him down, in his own person, in an Arcadian cave. He is not addressed outside the context of the poem, as Pollio, Varus, and Octavian were previously, nor is he merely spoken of, as he was in the "Song of Silenus" in *Eclogue* 6. He is a figure on the landscape as much as Tityrus or Menalcas or Daphnis. In fact he is treated as if he *were* Daphnis, dying of unfulfilled love. It is as if Virgil wanted to push his own conventions to their limit before he left them. And in Gallus he had a historical figure from outside the pastoral world to represent virtually all of his pastoral themes: Gallus, the handsome Celt, about the same age as Virgil, was his close friend (perhaps, some infer from *Eclogue* 10, his *love*); he was he most promising poet of the day, still experimenting but very much the hope for a Golden Age of *poetry*; he was, however, drawn—fatally as it turned out—to the *city*, its politics and its wars. And in this last eclogue he has come to a crisis, and thinks perhaps Arcadia can shelter him and provide him with some perspective.

It seems that, in his four books of elegiac love lyrics, the *Amores* now unfortunately lost to us, Gallus had written of his being forsaken by the beautiful Lycoris, the woman generally identified as the actress Cytheris, former mistress of Junius Brutus and Mark Antony and represented in the eclogue as following yet another soldier across the Alps. Virgil makes the personal crisis a metaphor for an artistic crisis: Gallus has lost the muse that inspired his poetry. (It is possible that Gallus has failed to rise to the task imposed on him in the "Song of Silenus" in *Eclogue* 6 where, in the midst of a catalogue of myths, Linus and the Muses gave him Hesiod's pipe and the commission to sing those myths in Alexandrian style.)

So, in *Eclogue* 10, Virgil represents Gallus as the dying Daphnis, stumbling into Arcadia, wept over by mountains and forests, sheep and shepherds, and visited, as was Theocritus' dying Daphnis, by three gods. Many of Virgil's lines may be (Servius[1] tells us that they are) paraphrases of Gallus' own verses, and the three visiting gods may as well be figures from Gallus' love poems, for each of them has, like Gallus, lost a beloved—Apollo his Daphne, Pan his Syrinx, Silvanus his Cypressis. But with the three gods, each lost love was transmuted into something pastoral and beautiful—flower or tree or musical instrument. Gallus, sadly, cannot reconcile himself to his loss or turn it to something creative and fruitful. He bids the Arcadians sing his sorrows so that he may die. He says he would have been able to survive had he become, like they, an Arcadian—that is to say, been able to deal with his emotions in symbolic figures on a landscape. For a while he entertains the thought of becoming an Arcadian, but that fantasy soon turns brusquely macho and unArcadian—hunting the wild boar with hounds on snowy mountain ridges, shooting with the savage arrows used in contemporary warfare by the Parthians. For a while too, Gallus thinks he can kill his erotic desires (for that is what the boar usually symbolizes) with the weapons of political and military commitment. But this is impossible in Arcadia.

In the end, Gallus sees that no landscape can give him release from his obsessions—not the wintry Hebrus (where, we remember, the poet Orpheus met his death), nor scorching Ethiopia (where, we remember, his own military career was eventually to bring him). Gallus finally submits to his passion in what, again, may be a quotation from his own verses:

> omnia vincit Amor: et nos cedamus Amori.

> Love conquers all. Let me too submit to Love.

This capitulation need only mean that Gallus will return, after an unsuccessful attempt at the pastoral mode, to his own genre, the elegiac love lyric. But it more likely means that, like the Daphnis in whose role he is cast, Gallus *dies* symbolically in Arcadia, his life as a poet effectively ended, his potential unfulfilled. Again, Virgil spells nothing out, and leaves us wondering.

Without any of Gallus' complete poems, we cannot feel our way very far into this last eclogue. (Some critics take it as essentially humorous!) What we can say is that, whether Gallus dies in Arcadia to write no more, or simply leaves it to return to his own genre, Virgil has, by placing a personal acquaintance halfway between real and imagined existence, distanced himself from his Arcadia for the first time. And from this new vantage point he has stated, one last time and more pessimistically than before, his pastoral themes — that music has only limited power in Arcadia; that both passionate love and the city over the hill can destroy; that the promise of the Golden Age may not, at least in the case of Gallus so honored by the Muses, be fulfilled. If it was Pollio who first suggested to Virgil that he begin the *Eclogues,* it was, somehow, Gallus who determined he would end them, and leave Arcadia.

But Gallus' "death" has not been for nothing. Like the death of Daphnis, it is ultimately fruitful. It brings peace and artistic completion to Virgil. As he ends his last eclogue, Virgil tells his Muses that his love for "Gallus, Gallus" has been "growing within him hour by hour." Far from being destructive, like the erotic passion felt by so many of his pastoral figures, this is a creative love. It is "like the green alder pushing upwards when spring is new":

> cuius amor tantum mihi crescit in horas

> quantum vere novo viridis se subicit alnus.

Now he sees the work he has done in a new way, and uses a small but memorable image to express it. His writing the *Eclogues* has been like weaving a shepherd's basket from mallow stalks:

> gracili fiscellam texit hibisco.

His book of "selections" is a work of art fashioned from nature, modest but intricately woven, and his own.

This signature image comes in an eight-line epilogue that balances the poem's eight-line prologue, addressed to the fresh-water nymph Arethusa who lives in the perpetual state of leaving Arcadia unscathed. Virgil too will leave. He must. He sees that the shade trees of Arcadia are, after a time, dangerous for poets.

In the end, with the Muses, the green alder pushing upwards, the sublimated love for Gallus, and the durable shepherd's basket of his own making (a reminiscence of the end of the eclogue he possibly wrote first, *Eclogue* 2), Virgil leaves his Arcadia. Perhaps he knows it will be granted him now to attempt the mission Gallus failed in—to move to a higher, Hesiodic world, to write the *Georgics*.

XII

Reading the Eclogues

We have had occasion, throughout the past chapters, to remark that Virgil did not compose the *Eclogues* in the order in which they were finally arranged. A possible order of composition, based on external events, cross-references within the poems, and stylistic considerations,[1] might be 2, 3, 5, 7, 8, 9, 1, 6, 4, 10—the first five written in response to Pollio's suggestion that Virgil become the Latin Theocritus, 9 and 1 resulting from Virgil's distress over the land confiscations, 4 expressing his optimism after the treaty of Brundisium, 6 and 10 composed some time apart from each other, when his hopes for Gallus were raised and then dashed. The composition, we are told in Servius and the Life of Virgil found in Donatus, spread over three years (so Virgil wrote, on the average, less than a line a day), and the years are generally thought to be those from 42 to 39 B.C.,[2] when the poet was in his late twenties and early thirties. The poems would have been read to or circulated among Virgil's friends, and possibly *that* is the reason why they came to bear the name *Eclogues*—as selections or excerpts from a contemplated cycle of poems, released singly or in small groups.[3]

It is likely that Virgil himself eventually arranged his poems for publication in the order in which we have them: the grammarian Probus indicates that this is so;[4] the order is consistently followed in the manuscript tradition, and references in the writings of Ovid, Calpurnius, and Virgil himself indicate that in antiquity the collection began with Tityrus (*Eclogue 1*).[5]

Any interpretation of the *Eclogues* as a whole must ask why Virgil placed the poems in their final positions. Readers of the *Georgics* and *Aeneid* will look first for an alternating pattern: books

101

1 and 3 of the *Georgics* (the "pessimistic" books) have one set of patterns, books 2 and 4 (the "optimistic") another; books 2, 4, and 6 of the *Aeneid* have from Virgil's day been regarded as the greatest, with 8, 10, and 12 achieving almost comparable status in recent years. (If Virgil's even-numbered books are the peaks and his odd-numbered the valleys, that marks him in one respect as the antitype to Beethoven, whose greatest symphonies are, by common consent, 1, 3, 5, 7, and 9—though I have always loved the sixth, the Pastoral, best). When Virgil has one of his shepherd judges remark *amant alterna Camenae*, "the Muses love songs that go back and forth," he may be commenting not only on amoebean verse but on his preference for arranging his work in contrasting sections on alternating levels of intent.

So we are not surprised, with the *Eclogues,* to find that numbers 1, 3, 5, 7, and 9 are dialogues, that numbers 2, 4, 6, 8, and 10 are monologues,[6] that Arcadia is mostly Mantua in the odd-numbered poems, mostly Sicily in the even. And though each of the eclogues has its champions, the even-numbered have on the whole received more attention (*Eclogue* 4 being on any count the most famous short poem in Latin) and more affection (again, I have always loved the sixth—at least the first part of it, about Silenus and the two faun-boys—best).

But the arrangement of the *Eclogues* is much more fascinating than a simple scheme of alteration. In the sequence 1, 3, 5, 7, 9 it is clear that numbers 1 and 9 are a pair (both deal with the land confiscations), and that 3 and 7 are a pair (both are contests of amoebean verse). In the sequence 2, 4, 6, 8, 10 it takes only a little analysis to see that 2 and 8 make a pair (both deal with unrequited love) as do 4 and 6 (both deal with oracular utterance). Finally, the poems unaccounted for in the two sequences, 5 and 10, correspond (both derive from Theocritus' first *Idyll*, on the death of Daphnis). The arrangement might be schematized thus:

```
              10
          1       9
        2           8
        3           7
          4       6
              5
```

These correspondences were first sighted in 1944 by Paul Maury[7] but not taken seriously at first by many critics,[8] partly because Maury, a Jesuit priest, described the ordering as a "chapelle bucolique" where Daphnis in *Eclogue* 5—a "pathetique et religieuse image" mourned by his "mère douloureuse"—is the centerpiece. Maury makes his way as a pilgrim, moving across his chapel from side altar to side altar, from *Eclogues* 1 to 9, 2 to 8, 3 to 7, 4 to 6, to arrive at Virgil's "heroön," *Eclogue* 5. *Eclogue* 10 is then set "a l'extremité de l'axe qui traverse le temple," an example of "l'amour profane" set against "l'amour sacré". Maury also noticed, rearranging the lines somewhat, that the chapel shaped itself into symmetrical proportions. But his good ideas were more or less lost in a welter of religious sentiment and unconvincing numerical considerations.

In 1969 Otto Skutsch, while insisting that the arrangement of the ten eclogues had no symbolic meaning, accepted Maury's floor plan, seeing it Virgil's purpose to center his edifice around the death and deification of Julius Caesar.[9] And he corrected Maury's numerical scheme in this interesting fashion:

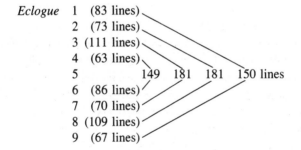

Eclogue 1 (83 lines)
2 (73 lines)
3 (111 lines)
4 (63 lines)
5   149   181   181   150 lines
6 (86 lines)
7 (70 lines)
8 (109 lines)
9 (67 lines)

This would be an impressive symmetrical arrangement indeed had Virgil thought to add one more line either to his "Messianic Eclogue" (4) or to his "Song of Silenus" (6). Skutsch went on to other demonstrations, sometimes convincing (the "Messianic Eclogue" is structured in groups of seven lines) and sometimes overly ingenious (*Eclogue* 2 is an A-B-C-D-C-B-A structure with the number of lines symmetrically equal—except that Virgil spoiled his scheme by adding eleven lines so as to make the poem, with its partner *Eclogue* 8, reach the requisite number of lines in the overall pattern).[10]

We ought not to dismiss Skutsch as a too systematic German (or, for that matter, to dismiss Maury as a too sentimental Frenchman). Their instincts are sound. Virgil had an Alexandrian's architectural sense, and it operated consciously or unconsciously throughout all his work.[11] It also seems reasonable to say, with William Berg, that he had an aesthetic eye for what copyists today call lay-out: "The appearance of the poems as they lay spread over the *volumen* (easily scanned when completely unrolled and held at arm's length) must indeed have been pleasing. The *Eclogues* would have appeared to grow and radiate out from *Eclogue* 5. Perhaps the finer editions were illuminated with simple pastoral motifs: perhaps the 'Daphnis' poem and the 'Gallus' poem had borders of ivy and acanthus to emphasize their relationship." (Berg also suggests that a shepherd's basket made of reeds such as Virgil, at the end of his *Eclogues,* uses as a metaphor for composition, "would spread up from the bottom in woven patterns of increasing complexity, so that the dominant structure would radiate out from a central configuration of crisscrossed reeds"—like the collection of eclogues itself.)[12]

Further, it seems necessary to say, a reader with a scroll would naturally read even a collection of poetry sequentially from beginning to end "with no skipping or dipping in."[13] John Van Sickle argues that a Roman reader was conditioned to "respond to sequential variation, enjoy the play of contrast in return of theme, admire a felicitous change, sense the import of positioning— proximities and deferrals, beginnings, articulations, ends."[14] For such a reader the ten individual eclogues would be no more autonomous than the movements of a Bach suite or a Mozart sonata. They would be more closely related, in fact, for characters recur from poem to poem, gathering associations with almost leitmotivic effect.

The young Virgil was writing in an Alexandrian tradition that, since Callimachus, had regarded such symmetries, and perhaps such sequences, as an essential part of its aesthetic. Even after he left Arcadia, Virgil still shaped his material as an Alexandrian. In the *Georgics* he framed his famous re-telling of the Orpheus myth within the theretofore unrelated myth of Aristaeus, in the manner of an Alexandrian epyllion, eventually achieving, in his onward-moving narrative, the pattern:

> A *Georgics* proper
> B   Aristaeus
>   C   Cyrene
>   D   Proteus
>   E   Orpheus and Eurydice
>   D   Proteus
>   C   Cyrene
> B   Aristaeus
> A   *Georgics* proper

Further, he tells his central Orpheus story in panels of seven lines that themselves form a symmetrical pattern within section E.[15]

Virgil may have been at work on the Aristaeus-Orpheus epyllion when he arranged the *Eclogues* in their final form. But we need not look forward to the *Georgics* to find a rationale for the architecture of the *Eclogues,* and a key to what they might mean. Some fifteen years before, Catullus wrote his poems 64 and 68.

Though Catullus is popularly known for his hundred-odd short poems in a variety of meters, and especially for the poems that detail his infatuation with the woman he called Lesbia, Catullus himself, and his circle of neoteric friends, clearly thought his and their great achievements lay in the longer poems in which they attempted various Alexandrian genres, and where the emotional content was stylized and patterned. The subject matter of these— Cinna's *Zmyrna,* Caecilius' *Magna Mater,* Calvus' *Io*—was myth, with special emphasis on the pathologically morbid and the grotesque. (The "Song of Silenus" in *Eclogue* 6, with its catalogue of savage, horrific mythological stories, probably details the subjects Gallus proposed to treat along these lines.) Catullus' most ambitious work in this genre, a work that we have already indicated Virgil knew well, was poem 64, in which two myths were told, one—the wedding of Peleus and Thetis—wreathed around the other—the desertion of Ariadne by Theseus—in the manner of an Alexandrian epyllion. On close examination Catullus' poem is shaped into a symmetrical structure than can be schematized thus:

A   The gods arrange the meeting of Peleus and Thetis

   B   Country folk flock into the wedding hall

      C   Ariadne

         D   Theseus

            E   Ariadne

         D   Theseus

      C   Ariadne

   B   Country folk leave the wedding hall

A   The gods celebrate the wedding of Peleus and Thetis

The heart of the poem, section E, is the long soliloquy spoken by Ariadne as she waits deserted on her island. Cross-references to the shorter poems suggest that Ariadne deserted by her lover speaks *mutatis mutandis* for the abandoned Catullus himself. In the outer parts of the poem, sections A and A, the poet deals with the wider theme of the divine impinging on human lives, a theme that by the end of his more-than-four-hundred-line poem has darkened considerably. In the first A section Catullus joyously salutes the past age when gods lived with men and filled them with grace; in the final A section he laments that the gods have, in his age, abandoned humankind to lives of depravity.

But the poem that influenced Virgil most as he arranged his eclogues in order was Catullus 68, an imperfectly realized work but an extraordinary conception, a kind of "personal epyllion" in which the poet's own crises are interlayed with the myths of the Trojan War in a series of symmetrically arranged panels exactly equal in length. Catullus begins poem 68 with an apology to his friend Allius[16] for being unable to write: he is far from Rome, in Verona, without his books and overwhelmed with grief. His brother has just died, far away near the site of ancient Troy. Then, to our surprise, the poem Catullus said he could not write begins, and it becomes clear that other crises have traumatized the poet— most immediately the successive revelations that Lesbia will always be faithless; that he is nonetheless lost without her (*odi et amo*); that the Roman ideals of *fides* and *pietas* which he once scorned are in fact more valuable by far than the life he has chosen, without family, without children; that true happiness is now beyond his grasp. At the center and heart of his poem is his sorrow at his brother's death (*fraterna mors*).

The intricate structure of poem 68 is as follows:

1–40   Apology: Catullus cannot write

   41–50   (10 lines)   Catullus expresses thanks to Allius
     51–56   (6 lines)   *Odi et amo*
       57–72   (16 lines)   Two similes; Lesbia
         73–86   (14 lines)   Laodamia
           87–90   (4 lines)   Troy
             91–100   *fraterna mors*
           101–104   (4 lines)   Troy
         105–118   (14 lines)   Laodamia
       119–136   (16 lines)   Two similes; Lesbia
     137–142   (6 lines)   *Odi et amo*
   143–152   (10 lines)   Catullus expresses thanks to Allius

153–160 Addendum: *huc addent*

What we have in poem 68 is an almost Freudian descent, through myth and poetic devices, from Catullus' self-absorbed feelings for the faithless Lesbia to a purer and more selfless emotion—the love he still has for his dead brother. Then, after facing that trauma at the center of the poet's feeling, we have a parallel ascent, a return journey taken in hope and determination. W.R. Johnson aptly describes the effect as "concentric circles of feeling and thought that drift towards a diminishing center: the self, again, parts of the self, dwindling to absence of self."[17]

The disappearance of virtually all of the epyllia of the Greek Alexandrians and of the "new" Latin Alexandrians of Catullus' circle makes it impossible to say how original poem 68 is. On the basis of what we know it seems absolutely unique, an extension of the epyllion from a myth-within-a-myth exercize, with emphasis on psychologizing the characters, to a deeply felt "personal epyllion," where the poet's own intimate experience, nakedly detailed, is made part of the concentric mythic spiral, where the poet himself is, as it were, the subject under analysis. The change made in the

genre is appropriately marked, in poem 68, by a change of meter—
from the epyllion's dactylic hexameter to the personal love lyric's
elegiac couplet.

When it came time for Virgil to publish his Alexandrian
"selections," he clearly decided to shape them into an Alexandrian
whole. He arranged his little pastorals into a series of concentric
circular patterns, and made the whole a kind of journey inwards
along the lines of Catullus 68. He arrangement begins and, if we
except for the moment *Eclogue* 10, ends with the immediate
traumatizing event in the poet's own experience, the confiscations
and evictions in his native Mantua, terrible in themselves and
emblematic of the chaotic times, the century of civil war in which
he lived. These are *Eclogues* 1 and 9. The poet then proceeds
inward to *Eclogues* 2 and 8, a matching pair in which Theocritus is
recognizable but strangely muted: comic Polyphemus wooing the
sea nymph becomes a pair of lovelorn herdsmen—Corydon in 2,
the suicidal goatherd in 8. And Virgil has moved from destructive
Ares in the outer circle inwards to destructive Eros—potentially
very destructive in the second part of 8.

In the next matching pair, the amoebean contests of 3 and 7,
Virgil moves inwards past the influence of the city (1 and 9) and
the madness of erotic love (2 and 8) to a kind of primitive
innocence; inwards from troubled Mantua (1 and 9) and lovelorn
Sicilia (2 and 8) to a blending of the two in happier circumstances,
to an Arcadia where the only wars are song competitions and the
only loves promiscuous but innocent dalliance.

Is such a childlike existence only a foolish dream when men are
beset from without by war and from within by uncontrollable passions? Virgil proceeds still further inwards with his most elaborate
pair of eclogues, the "Messianic Eclogue" and the "Song of Silenus,"
Eclogues 4 and 6, the former predicting that war will end and that the
flaw in human nature will be undone, the latter suggesting, on the
contrary, that human nature is fundamentally flawed, that the process
of deterioration, once begun, cannot be halted.

We begin to note that, of the pairs, the eclogues placed in the
second half of the collection are less hopeful than those in the first
half. Virgil grows increasingly pessimistic: there is some
exemption from eviction in 1, none in 9; unrequited love ends in
resignation and a return to creativity in 2, with suicide and delusion

in 8; the singing apprentices break even in 3, while the singing masters are unevenly matched and widely divergent in 7; the human race looks forward to a bright future in 4, deteriorates frightenly in 6. Catullus grew increasingly hopeful on his return journey from the central realization in poem 68. This is not true of Virgil, who is less hopeful as he moves past his center.

At the center of both poets' arrangements is death: the actual death of the brother and the symbolic death of Daphnis. The death in Catullus seems to have been ultimately an experience from which the poet grew, and from which he moved towards a reassessment of his life and his art. The death at the center of the *Eclogues* has no such hopeful effect on Virgil, even though it is immediately countered, within *Eclogue* 5, by an apotheosis—or, to use the term most appropriate to Virgil's work as a whole, by a rebirth. It is about the possibility of rebirth that Virgil grows increasingly pessimistic. And here is where we can relate the *Eclogues* to the two great Virgilian works that followed.

The possibility of rebirth is a major Virgilian theme. It lies at the heart and center of the *Aeneid*. In Book 6 of that massive poem, in the land of the dead, Virgil explains the nature of the world in terms of a world soul, and the nature of individual human existence in terms of the transmigration of souls. Book 6 thus provides at least a partial answer to the great Virgilian questions asked at the *Aeneid*'s beginning: "Why do the innocent suffer?" (*tot volvere casus / insignem pietate virum*) and "What is god?" (*tantaene animis caelestibus irae*). Suffering, the center of the poem suggests, is part of a cosmic, millenial plan for personal purification and rebirth. God is the force directing the process.

Death and rebirth are also the concern of the Orpheus-Aristaeus epyllion that, in mythic terms, explains the *Georgics*. Aristaeus' swarm of bees dies but is regenerated, reborn, when he pays due sacrifice to the spirit of Orpheus, whose story is told at the epyllion's center.

Rebirth is a concern of Virgil because he is a truly committed political poet, pondering in all three of his major works the possibility of humankind rising from the ashes of the wars of his century, wondering "Will the new Aeneas be able to lead his people from the fallen republic to a new empire? Will the new Aristaeus be able to restore the lost civilization symbolized by the lost swarm of bees? Will the new Daphnis be able, in his reforms, to bring back to life Italy's fields devastated by years of war and years of neglect? Will Octavian, become Caesar Augustus, be able to end the century of civil war? Will he find some way to stem the seemingly inevitable moral deterioration of his people? Or is the human race fundamentally flawed?"

It is possible to find positive, optimistic answers to these questions in Virgil's three works: Aeneas, strengthened by visions of the future, leads his people to the promised land of Italy; Aristaeus, acknowledging his debt to the intuitive artist Orpheus, restores life to his hive; Daphnis dies as Julius Caesar but is reborn as Octavian to become Caesar Augustus.

It is also possible to find negative, pessimistic answers in Virgil's three works. At the end of the *Aeneid* Aeneas, destroying his enemy, betrays the *pietas* that made him a hero and yields to the *furor* that he had always opposed. At the end of the *Georgics,* while Aristaeus is successful in bringing back to life the little civilization whose god he is, Orpheus fails tragically to resurrect his lost Eurydice. And, to come finally in our patterns to the end of the *Eclogues,* Virgil balances his dead-and-risen Daphnis in *Eclogue* 5 with his failed and despairing Daphnis-Gallus in *Eclogue* 10, the pessimism of which is prepared for by the darkening of the themes of *Eclogues* 4, 3, 2, and 1 in *Eclogues* 6, 7, 8, and 9.

Once he has passed the hopeful center of his pastoral-turned-personal epyllion, Virgil's sense of humanity as tragically flawed, strongest in the *Aeneid* but already clouding his outlook in the *Eclogues,* takes over. His ten-poem structure ends ambivalently. He acknowledges, in the failure of Gallus, the flaw in nature. But then, with the woven basket, the alder tree shooting upwards, and the hope that the Muses will make his poems endure as something *maxima Gallo,* something that will have "great meaning for Gallus," he determines to continue his creative role as poet. By the end of the *Eclogues,* Virgil has discovered what we might call the secret of Arcadia—that if a man projects himself beyond his immediate problems to an imaginary land of peace, he will find that the sources of disorder lie not so much without, in the wars that come from the city beyond his pleasance, as more fundamentally within that pleasance, in the depths of his own soul. It is *saepibus in nostris* that the *malus error* can be most clearly seen (*vidi . . . vidi*).

If we broaden the perspective, and see the *Eclogues* not just as Virgil's journey into himself, but as his meditation on the world of his time, we can see that world, now in effect ruled from one center, Rome, as having reached a moment of crisis. With the death of Julius Caesar and the emergence of Octavian as his successor (the central *Eclogue* 5), the world is open to two possible developments: there can be progress towards a Golden Age, symbolized in *Eclogue* 4 by the new-born child and the world renewing itself, or there can be a reversion to more destruction, symbolized in *Eclogue* 6 by the depravity in the myths there, and the world in decline and disintegrating. There can be reconciliation, a humble acknowledgement of man's ambivalence, expressed in *Eclogue* 3 by the contest tie and in *Eclogue* 2 by the lovesick Corydon's modestly re-assuming his duties, or there can be strife and a further unleashing of man's potential for destructiveness, expressed in *Eclogue* 7 by the uneven contest and in *Eclogue* 8 by the suicide of the lovesick man and the delusion of the lovesick woman. Rome can exercise its power benevolently, through the peace-giving young ruler in *Eclogue* 1, or with brutal force, through its barbarous legions in *Eclogue* 9.

In short, the *Eclogues* can be thought to dramatize, not just the anxieties of a young poet, but the ambivalences he sees in a great moment in history, a moment not unlike our own in this century, when we find ourselves morally unequipped to deal with the immense instruments of destruction we have in our hands: will the human race destroy itself in more wars, or will there be a movement upwards to reconciliation and peace? Are the tensions, the forces and counterforces in the world, set to destroy it? Is there a chance for rebirth?

Through all of his works, Virgil's symbolic answers are as ambivalent as his questions. The *Aeneid* leaves everything hanging fire, as Aeneas stands over his slain enemy filled with savage feelings, permanently compromised. The *Georgics* end with an emblem of civilization, Aristaeus' beehive, restored to life but, on a deeper level, with Orpheus' Eurydice permanently lost to him. And the *Eclogues*, centered on the promise of Daphnis' death and apotheosis, end with the failure of the Daphnis-figure Gallus to find peace with himself. In the three works Aeneas, Aristaeus, an Daphnis-in-apotheosis can easily symbolize the one man in Rome, Octavian-become-Augustus, who is powerful enough to restore the world. In each case, Virgil feels anxiety, if not despair, as that man faces the future.

But in fact, the promising but ruthless Octavian eventually did, as a confident and benevolent Augustus, rebuild Rome, restore the land to fertility, and give the world peace. Virgil was more wary of him, more pessimistic about human nature, than he needed to be. Virgil remained, from the *Eclogues* through the *Georgics* to the *Aeneid,* a true Arcadian, not a Utopian. He saw human nature as fundamentally flawed (that is Arcadia's secret), not as perfect or perfectible (that is Utopia's dream). The Arcadian view is the truer one. The Arcadian knows that there are no permanent answers to man's never-ending problems, but that an awareness of his potential for good and evil can keep his problems in perspective; that passion, ever manifest in human events as destructive, can be controlled and, outwardly directed as love, put to creative ends; that poetry is not a remedy for suffering but is in fact born out of suffering and chiefly valuable as a means of self-understanding.

In Virgil's final arrangement of his ten pastoral poems, then, we may read him as saying:

Eclogue 1: Rome, at this point in history, has the power to give the world war or peace.

Eclogue 2: Love, the force that animates the world, has both creative and destructive potential.

Eclogue 3: Art, the symbolic expression of human nature, is at least partly accessible to ordinary men.

Eclogue 4: The world could be poised on the brink of a rebirth; myth tells of a Golden Age.

Eclogue 5: We have lost Julius Caesar, but he has been reborn in Augustus Caesar.

Eclogue 6: The world could be set on a downward spiral; myth tells of a flaw in human nature.

Eclogue 7: Art is the symbolic expression of our ambivalences; the art of one exceptional man is inaccessible to another.

Eclogue 8: Love, potentially creative, is more often destructive or illusory.

Eclogue 9: Rome, with the power to rule justly, acts unjustly.

Eclogue 10: I have lost Gallus, but found my true nature in the ambivalences these eclogues have shown me are a part of myself.

XIII

Interpreting the Eclogues: Eclogue 6

The impulse that sends a man to Arcadia, the flight from his Mausoleum Club back into the past to re-create in imagination his own childhood, to find there the innocence he once knew and has since lost, is fundamentally a desire to be reborn. In these final pages I shall have recourse, as I had in my book on Virgil's *Aeneid,* to some of the ideas of Carl Jung, always illuminating when brought to bear on the work of intuitive artists like Virgil.

In his paper "Concerning Rebirth," Jung describes the desire for rebirth as one of mankind's primordial urges, manifested in such archetypes as the risen hero.[1] Jung cites the "perfect symbol" of Jesus, and the other instances of Dionysus and Khidr. Paul's experience of Jesus dead and risen, Nietzsche's vision of Dionysus-Zagreus dismembered and reborn, and Moses' encounter, in the Koran, with Khidr reincarned from the fish he intended to eat, are all transforming experiences. Jesus appears on a journey, Dionysus at the hour sacred to Pan, Khidr from a cave—all of them situations familiar from the *Eclogues.* And after the encounters Paul, Nietzsche, and Moses are all, in a spiritual sense, reborn.[2]

Daphnis dying and reborn is such a symbol for Virgil, a symbol explored in its many primitive manifestations in Sir James George Frazer's massive compendium of comparative mythology, *The Golden Bough,* and still active and alive, if we credit the analytical psychologists, in the human psyche. In primitive tribes the old king or priest is ritually killed and the new leader crowned to ensure the continuation of the crop cycle. In the unchanging psyche of man, small transforming deaths are also commanded by nature. ("Except a corn of wheat fall into the ground and die, it abideth alone: but if it die, it bringeth forth much fruit.") In Virgil's imagination, and central to it, is the death of the old ruler and his re-emergence transformed, the death of Julius Caesar and the emergence of Octavian in the central figure of Daphnis. It is even possible to say, with *Eclogue* 5 prefaced by the prophetic *Eclogue* 4, that the divine child promised in the messianic poem is Daphnis reborn in the next poem, for both the return of the Golden Age and the apotheosis of Daphnis are myths reworked by, concepts new with, Virgil.

What, then, of the other eclogues? Transformations within the psyche announce themselves in clear, related symbols. One of these, Jung finds, is the emergence of "the other person in ourselves—that larger and greater personality maturing within us . . . that inner friend of the soul into whom Nature herself would like to change us." So Virgil's imagined inner world is a world of dialogues. In the *Eclogues,* we read not just the amoebean exchanges we expect in an art derived from Theocritus and ultimately from shepherds' songs. We read dialogues which are attempts at self-understanding in the face of crisis (Tityrus and Meliboeus, Lycidas and Moeris on the land confiscations), or projections of immortality out of mortality (Menalcas and Mopsus on Daphnis dead and risen) or disputations on the purposes of poetry (art vs. nature in Menalcas and Damoetas, Apollonian vs. Dionysian in Corydon and Thyrsis). The two "halves" of Virgil converse. "We are," Jung says, "that pair of Dioscuri, one of whom is mortal and the other immortal," and if the two within us are not always in harmony, still "the conflict between them may give rise to truth and meaning."[3]

Writers on the pastoral have always seen its conventions as a means to such ends, though of course their language is not so clinical as Jung's: "The assumption of the shepherd's weeds and the entrance into Arcadias of the mind reveals that a poet can conceive of two ways at least of looking at himself and at reality." The sensitive writer of those words actually finds himself, for a moment, psychologizing: "The sympathy for other ways of life and thought, the capacity for self-appraisal, the lack of rigidity in the personality implied by such a gesture all augur well for the future development of the personality. Part-playing is a necessary part of all life, though a mind of puritanical cast will frequently see it as evidence of a lack of integrity: witness the modern emphasis on simple 'sincerity' . . . To be able to imagine several positions rather than one is the hallmark of a larger and more buoyant mind and of a more engaging personality as well."[4]

Virgil's divine child of *Eclogue* 4 is an archetype which Jung finds in such other manifestations as Meister Eckhart's vision of the "naked boy" and Goethe's Faust transformed into a child and admitted to the "choir of blessed youths" before becoming, at the end, Doctor Marianus.[5] The child in these instances represents the pre-conceived aspect of an individual or of the world itself, and recurs at times when the image-making subject, man or world, has lost touch with the past and anxiously anticipates future developments. The miraculous events that accompany the appearance of this archetype (the spontaneous flowering of nature in Virgil's poem) signify that the child's is a psychic, not a physical, birth. The dangers that surround him at birth (the serpent, the poison flower) show how precarious is the possibility of his surviving to grow ultimately to manhood and fruition, to effect in the psyche that wholeness which is his mission. The motif of "smaller than small yet bigger than big" (cf. Virgil's antithesis *parve puer / magnum incrementum*) attests to the real possibility of his eventual triumph. The development of child to young hero (Virgil's *puer* reading about his father, and going about his father's business) represents the emergence of the idea, born in the unconscious, into consciousness. The dawning of light at his birth (Virgil's *casta fave Lucina: tuus iam regnat Apollo*) is the projection of that first evolutionary step, the coming of consciousness. Psychologically speaking, the child in *Eclogue* 4 is an idea born, nurtured, and blossoming in Virgil's personal, and in the world's collective, unconscious.

Finally, as more and more of Virgil's figures come to be aspects of the poet himself, we can say that what Jung calls the individuation process—the attempt of the unconscious to solve its problems—is seen in outline in the *Eclogues,* eventually to receive detailed treatment in the *Georgics* and the *Aeneid.* In literature the process is best expressed in the myth of the hero—his encounter, in some place which represents his unconscious, first with his *anima* or feminine side, then with his masculine "Wise Old Man" archetype, and his final integration of these two experiences, upon his return to consciousness, in his Self—usually symbolized in some object or design (Jung's mandala) in which the unconscious tensions are held in centripetal balance. The hero myth is essentially the myth of the maturing male.

Virgil's best known example of this is his hero's journey to his dead father, aided by his goddess mother, in Book 6 of the *Aeneid:* Aeneas passes through two parts of the unconscious—from a moon-lit, potentially destructive and partly illusory *anima* to a sun-lit area in which his wise old father shows him his future, and the secrets of rebirth, in a field of light. The hero of the *Aeneid* seems, however, not successfully to complete his individuation process: he returns to consciousness by the gate of false dreams, never remembers (certainly never refers to) his underworld journey thereafter, does not know what the figures on his mandala-like shield mean, and on the last page of his poem forgets the injunction his father gave him ("spare the suppliant"). Aeneas remains something of a failed hero, caught between *pietas* and *furor,* his world-view of *anima* (Juno) and wise old man (Jupiter) gone utterly awry.[6]

Then there is an example of a successfully completed individuation process in the little hero myth Virgil tells in the epyllion at the close of the *Georgics.* The young shepherd god, Aristaeus, loses his swarm of bees to disease and famine and sues for help to his mother Cyrene at the bottom of her river. The watery realm strongly suggests the feminine *anima,* with its bevy of eighteen water nymphs singing all the tales of birthing since creation, its wave curving like a mountain above the young god to take him to its bosom, its picturesque underwater cave hung with stalactites, its subaqueous libations of wine and sacrifices of fire. In this *anima*-world, the mother knows that her son has nothing to fear, but cannot tell him what he must know. That he must find out for himself, from the Wise Old Man.

The mother conducts her son to another cave, in the side of a mountain where wind-driven waves break into receding circles (a marvelously evocative image of the unconscious). She hides him there, and retires wrapped in a mist as Aristaeus awaits the arrival of Proteus, the wise old man who herds Neptune's seals, who can change to all manner of shapes, and must be pinned down and compelled to reveal his secrets. The atmosphere in this second encounter with an archetype—the Dog Star blazing, the fiery sun reaching mid-course, scorching the grass and drying the rivers—is symbolically opposed to the sheltering, watery realm of the *anima*. We have moved from the dark intuitive feminine to the blazing bright and rational masculine.

Proteus comes with his seals and, like a shepherd, counts them and settles down with them for his noontime sleep. Aristaeus seizes the moment and clasps the wise old man fast.

But none of the sealherd's protean tricks can work because the mother has anointed her son with ambrosia. So finally Proteus, his eyes blazing with light, tells Aristaeus why his bees have died: Orpheus has sent the plague on them because, when Aristaeus once made advances to Eurydice, she fled him only to step on the serpent that sent her to her death. Orpheus was able with his song to bring Eurydice back from death. But then he lost her again through his own human frailty—and it was he, Aristaeus, who with erotic passion began all this sorrow.

Proteus, the story told, dives abruptly into the sea and vanishes beneath the swirl. So the wise old man reveals the knowledge that the hero lacks (the sin for which he must atone). But that knowledge must, in the individuation process, be integrated with the *anima* before it becomes redemptive and creative. And Aristaeus' mother is instantly there to tell him what he must do. The requisite sacrifices are performed and, lo!, swarming from the bodies of the sacrificed animals ("Except a corn of wheat fall into the ground and die . . .") are the young god's bees reborn. As they fly aloft, Virgil even provides, in the unusual phrase *uvam demittere* ("they hung in a grape-like cluster") a mandala-figure to satisfy the strictest Jungian.

Much the same pattern is adumbrated in the most delightful passage in all of the *Eclogues,* the narrative that leads to the song of Silenus in *Eclogue 6:*

> Pergite, Pierides. Chromis et Mnasyllos in antro
> Silenum pueri somno videre iacentem,
> inflatum hesterno venas, ut semper, Iaccho;
> serta procul tantum capiti delapsa iacebant
> et gravis attrita pendebat cantharus ansa.
> adgressi (nam saepe senex spe carminis ambo

luserat) iniciunt ipsis ex vincula sertis.
addit se sociam timidisque supervenit Aegle,
Aegle Naiadum pulcherrima, iamque videnti
sanguineis frontem moris et tempora pingit.
ille dolum ridens "quo vincula nectitis?" inquit;
"solvite me, pueri; satis est potuisse videri.
carmina quae vultis cognoscite; carmina vobis,
huic aliud mercedis erit." simul incipit ipse.

Forward, ye Muses! Chromis and Mnasyllus, when they were
just boys, saw Silenus in a cave, lying fast asleep.
Yesterday's wine, as always, swelled his veins. His garlands
lay nearby, just slipped from his head, and his tankard
still hung, heavy, by the handle he had almost worn thin.
The boys sprang on him—for the old man had often
eluded them both, after raising their hopes with a promise
of song—and they cast upon him chains made from his
own garlands. Then, as they stood still afraid of him,
Aegle came running up and added herself to their company.
Aegle was fairest of all the Naiads. And just as Silenus
opened his eyes, she got his forehead and temples painted
with blood-red mulberry juice. He laughed when he saw
they had tricked him, and asked, "Why have you bound me
with wreaths? Let me go, lads. I was caught when you
first saw me. That was enough.[7] The songs you want—
listen to them now. There'll be songs for you lads,
and for the lass here a different reward." And he started to sing.

Here we have two young heroes—two appropriately, as the
Eclogues are largely an inner world of dialogue[8]—and from all
indications they are not shepherds but forest fauns.[9] They are aided
by the *anima*-figure Aigle, who arrives just in time to smear the
wise old man's face with apotropaeic mulberry juice that will
enable them to look on him without suffering harm.[10] The male
embodiment of wisdom is in this instance a full-bodied, lecherous
satyr, the famous tutor and servant of Bacchus, filled with the wine
of that god's daemonic spirit but, when its effect has been slept off,
skilled too in the creative songs of Apollo (as is made clear when
his song is done). Half Apollonian, half Dionysian, he is also
half-man, half-animal—hence a source of complete wisdom,
reason and instinct both, if only he can be caught.

His binding by the two boys represents not just the attempt to capture nature and force it to sing but their need to know what lies within the nature they, as fauns, share with the animals: the quest for the Wise Old Man is always a quest for self-knowledge. (The reader may also want to suppose, with Servius, that the situation corresponds to the young Virgil's learning, with one of his fellow students, from their Epicurean master Siro. He will almost certainly think of Socrates in Plato's *Symposium:* young Alcibiades there wreathes his teacher's head with a garland, asks for a speech, adds that he has always found Socrates elusive, and compares him to Silenus—grossness without, wisdom and beauty of soul within.[11])

So Silenus sings, and we hear in wonder how creation began when the first elements were driven through the void, how the globe shaped itself, the seas and lands separating, how the earth gazed in amazement at the sun, how showers fell and forests rose, and living creatures appeared here and there among the mountains, wondering what the world meant.

Then the Silenus song touches briefly on a series of myths: man's first blissful existence, his original sin and the punishment for it, the repeopling of the earth after the flood. From there, with the cry of the sailors for the drowned Hylas echoing in our ears, we are plunged into a fleeting account of the most savage and degrading of man's myths. Perhaps they are only meant to be an Alexandrian catalogue of the morbid subjects favored by Callimachus (his *Aitia* is quoted in the opening of the eclogue) and then, as we have suggested before, chosen by Gallus for treatment in Latin. But when the "Song of Silenus" is fitted into its place in the collection, as a companion piece to the optimistic "Messianic Eclogue," the feeling inevitably is that the pathological myths— Pasiphae's mating with the bull, the daughters of Proetus maddened into thinking they are cattle, Atalanta obsessed with love's apples, Phaethon's sisters turned to trees for a sin of hybris, Scylla turned for lust into a sea monster, Tereus and his wife Philomel turned to birds after his brutal rape of her sister and her tricking him to eat his own son's flesh—are all intended as a reversal of the wondrous creation earlier in the song, as a destructive downward spiral back into chaos to set against the optimistic upward movement of the companion poem, the "Messianic Eclogue".

Such, at any rate, is the song that the jocular half-animal man offers to the two listening half-animal boys: humankind, flawed by its original sin and prone to evil, has steadily given way to the animal in its nature. This is also the song, we learn at the poem's end, that Apollo once sang at the river where, accidentally killing his beloved Hyacinthus, he knew at first hand of beauty destroyed. Nature herself is shaken by the song, and sends it back to the starry void where creation began. We are not told what the two boys thought of the revelation—the discovery that the animal passions within them have such destructive potential. But we know why Silenus was reluctant to yield his secret. We are left with the sole hope that Gallus, singing these same myths with his special mandate, will find a way to mend the flaw in human nature.

Virgil offers *Eclogue* 6 as a cautionary tale to anyone *captus amore*, caught by love (line 10). And then, when we come to the end of his *Eclogues*, it is Gallus himself, the one chosen to interpret the myths, who is caught by love; the flaw in nature remains uncorrected.

But at least Virgil has seen that the flaw is there. Arcadia has revealed it to him. And once the separate pieces, the ten "selections," are fitted into their appropriate places in his structure, we find that Virgil has achieved something of the synthesis expected from Gallus: the song of the *anima*-Sibyl in *Eclogue* 4 is held in tension by the song of the Wise-Old-Man-Silenus in *Eclogue* 6, and the promise of birth in the one and the reversion to chaos in the other cut across the death and rebirth of Daphnis in the eclogue between them. And all of this stands at the center of meditations on the power of poetry (3 and 7), the tyranny of love (2 and 8), and the sufferings of humanity (1 and 9). In the end, when Gallus has failed to effect such a synthesis, Virgil quietly leaves his Arcadia with the knowledge that he has done something of what Gallus was asked to do, something *maxima Gallo*. We feel that he has come to the knowledge, especially the self-knowledge, that such an inward journey should bring.

The image that remains in the mind as we close the book is another mandala to satisfy any Jungian, an emblem to satisfy any literary critic—a shepherd's basket intricately woven of pliant reeds. A work of art made from carefully selected parts. And an image of wholeness.

Notes

I Mariposa

1. "Preface to the Original Edition," *Sunshine Sketches of a Little Town* (Toronto, 1984, repr.), n.p. The essays cited may be found, respectively, in *Behind the Beyond* (1913), *Too Much College* (1939), and *The Boy I Left Behind Me* (1946, posthumous). A choice quote from "Homer and Humbug": "I know there are solid arguments advanced in favor of the classics. I often hear them from my colleagues. My friend the professor of Greek tells me that he truly believes the classics have made him what he is. This is a very grave statement, if well founded. Indeed, I have heard the same argument from a great many Latin and Greek scholars. They all claim, with some heat, that Latin and Greek have practically made them what they are. This damaging charge against the classics should not be too readily accepted. In my opinion some of these men would have been what they are, no matter what they were."

2. John Stevens, "Introduction" *Sunshine Sketches,* n.p. For a similar response to Arcadian literature during a more recent war, see Charles Segal: "Is it coincidental that the remarkable efflorescence of studies of the *Eclogues* and the strongest new directions in approaches to ancient pastoral in the United States came when we were involved in a costly, unpopular, and divisive war?" (*Poetry and Myth in Ancient Pastoral* [Princeton, 1981], p. 7).

3. It is impossible to say in what part of war-torn Italy Virgil composed his *Eclogues*. Following Edward Coleiro, *An Introduction to Vergil's Bucolics* (Amsterdam, 1979) and the survey of opinions he provides (see especially p. 93), we can make a case for *Eclogues* 2, 3, and 5 being written in Mantua, 7, 8, 9, 1, 4, and 6 in Rome, and 10 in Naples.

II Sicilia

1. The only predecessors mentioned (by Athenagoras 14.619, Diodorus 4.84, and Aelian *Vera Historia* 10.18) are the mythical figures Diomus and Daphnis.

2. *Deipnosophistae* 5.25. More details than are given here may be found in Andrew Lang's introductory essay in *Theocritus, Bion and Moschus* (London, 1913), pp. xxx–xxxvi.

3. For a full discussion of this matter, see David M. Halperin, *Before Pastoral* (Yale, 1983), pp. 8–16.

4. The collection seems also to have contained some of the work of Theocritus' successors in the pastoral genre—Moschus from the middle and Bion from the end of the second century B.C. Moschus' main concern is erotic love, Bion's death. Bion's longest poem, a lament for Adonis, prompted a famous *Lament for Bion*, written at his death by an anonymous author.

5. Steven F. Walker, in *Theocritus* (Boston, 1980), pp. 126–7, sees Callimachus as paying tribute to the pastoral in epigram 24.

6. Gilbert Lawall, in *Theocritus' Coan Pastorals: A Poetry Book* (Cambridge, Mass., 1967), sees the first seven idylls as written on Cos and designed to form a unified whole. The interesting thesis has not, however, won complete scholarly support.

7. Though Virgil's century thought that Idylls VIII and IX were by Theocritus, their authenticity is doubted today. See, e.g., L. E. Rossi, "Mondo Pastorale e Poesia Bucolica di Maniera" *Studi Italiani di Filologia Classica* 43 (1971), pp. 5–25, with bibliography.

8. The differences between Homer and Theocritus are succinctly detailed in Halperin, *Before Pastoral*, p. 254.

9. Gavin Maxwell, *The Ten Pains of Death* (London, 1959), pp. 46–50. I owe my acquaintance with Maxwell to A. G. McKay's affectionate traversal of the poet's outer landscape, *Vergil's Italy* (London, 1971).

10. For the *locus amoenus* as an essential part of the pastoral see E. R. Curtius, *European Literature and the Latin Middle Ages*, tr. W. R. Trask (London, 1953), p. 192.

III   Mantua

1. The details from the various ancient *Vitae* of Virgil are not easy, and often impossible, to substantiate; many of them seem to have been deduced by the early commentators Donatus, Servius, and Probus from the poems themselves. A reconstruction of Virgil's life based on good

evidence can be found in Edward Coleiro, *An Introduction to Vergil's Bucolics* (Amsterdam, 1979), pp. 3–9. I have used it extensively here.

2. The farm may have belonged to Virgil's mother's family, and have been a rather extensive estate. See Coleiro (above, note 1), p. 3.

3. It is reasonably certain that Gaius Asinius Pollio is the young Pollio Catullus refers to in 12.8–9 as *leporum / disertus puer ac facetiarum*. See T. P. Wiseman, *Catullan Questions* (Leicester, 1969), pp. 38–9.

4. See the *Vita Serviana* 23–4: *tunc ei proposuit Pollio ut carmen bucolicum scriberet*.

5. Catullus 30 is almost surely addressed to him. (It is not impossible but quite unlikely that the Varus mentioned in *Eclogue* 6 is Quintilius Varus, a fellow student with Virgil and Gallus at the school of Siro. Horace describes him in his *Ars Poetica* 438–44 and *Odes* 1.24 as an incorruptible critic with the highest standards.)

6. Apart from Virgil's *homages* to him in *Eclogues* 6 and 10, Ovid bears witness to his genius in *Amores* 3.9.59–66 and *Tristia* 4.10.53–4.

7. In addition to the pentameter line *uno tellures dividit amne tuas*, preserved in the geographer Vibius Sequester, we now have fragments of four poems (ten whole or partly preserved lines) from Egyptian Nubia. See R. D. Anderson, P. J. Parsons, and R. G. M. Nisbet, "Elegiacs by Gallus from Qasr Ibrim" *JRS* 69 (1979), pp. 125–55. David O. Ross, scrutinizing the pre-1979 evidence in *Backgrounds to Augustan Poetry: Gallus, Elegy and Rome* (Cambridge, 1975), concludes on p. 46 that "Gallus wrote four books of elegies, and nothing more". His arguments are brilliant but unconvincing.

8. P. A. Brunt, "The Army and the Land in the Roman Revolution" *JRS* 59 (1962), p. 69.

9. See Horace *Satires* 2.2.112–36 and *Epistles* 2.2.49–52; Tibullus 1.1.19–23; Propertius 4.1.127–30.

10. There have always been critics who, unable to credit the *Vitae*, have held that Virgil never lost his property or interceded directly on behalf of the Mantuans. See, in recent years, Robert Coleman's excellent edition, *Vergil: Eclogues* (Cambridge, 1977), pp. 89–90 and 274–5. Certainly Servius and the other early commentators were overly zealous in reading autobiographical details into the poems. I can only say that I am

aware of the dangers of the course I have taken here, and have tried not to force the poems and the historical facts together.

11. See Brunt (above, note 8), p. 82.

12. See *Eclogue* 10.2–3, 44–5. On internal evidence, the poem seems best assigned to the year 37 B.C., when Agrippa led an expedition across the Alps and up the Rhine to the region eventually to become Cologne.

13. See Servius on 3.94 (*non bene ripas / creditur*): *post acceptos agros, ab Arrio centurione paene est interemptus, nisi se praecipitasset in fluvium*. The *Vita Donatiana* (63) gives full details: *sed Vergilius merito carminum fretus et amicitia quorundam potentium centurioni Arrio cum obsistere ausus esset, ille statim, ut miles, ad gladium manum admovit, cumque se in fugam proripuisset poeta, non prius finis persequendi fuit, quam se in fluvium Vergilius coniecisset atque ita in alteram ripam enatavisset.*

14. See *Vita Donatiana* 26: *eo successu edidit, ut in scena quoque per cantores crebro pronuntiarentur*. Henry Bardon, in his review of Jean Granarolo: *D'Ennius à Catulle, Gnomon* 44 (1972), p. 258, accepts this, and Günther Wille, in *Einführung in das Römische Musikleben* (Darmstadt, 1977), p. 115 fn. 303, calls the opposition to it "unnötig skeptisch". Servius' comment on *Eclogues* 6.11, to the effect that Cicero met Virgil after such a performance cannot, however, by any stretch of chronology be accepted.

IV   Arcadia

1. Bruno Snell, "Arcadia: The Discovery of a Spiritual Landscape," from *The Discovery of the Mind*, tr. T. G. Rosenmeyer (Oxford, 1953), p. 281. The essay has come under some criticism in the last decade for making too clear a distinction between a realistic pastoral world in Theocritus and a dreamy never-never one in Virgil.

2. The present-day notion of pastoral Arcadia owes much to post-Virgilian details added by Jacopo Sannazaro (*Arcadia*, 1481) and Sir Philip Sidney (*Arcadia*, 1580).

3. John Van Sickle, noting that Arcadia is mentioned specifically only in Eclogues 4, 7, and 10, reads the poems sequentially as Virgil's gradual realization of his Arcadian ideal. See *The Design of Virgil's Bucolics* (Rome, 1978), pp. 71–2.

4. D. E. W. Wormell, "The Originality of the Eclogues" in D. R. Dudley ed., *Virgil* (London, 1969), p. 14.

5. Viktor Pöschl, speaking of the *Aeneid* in *The Art of Virgil* (tr. Gerda Seligson [Ann Arbor, 1970], p. 15), quotes pertinently from Goethe: "Symbolic objects are outstanding cases representing in their variety many others," and Hebbel: "Every genuine work of art is a mysterious symbol with many meanings, to a certain degree incomprehensible".

6. Peter V. Marinelli, *Pastoral* (London, 1971), p. 3.

7. Paul Alpers, in *The Singer of the Eclogues* (Berkeley, 1979), rightly places Theocritus among Schiller's "naive" to match Virgil among his "sentimental" poets, citing (p. 244) "Virgil's deep understanding that any representation—at least for a latter-day 'sentimental' poet—is a self-representation."

8. In *Eclogue* 1.53–8, Tityrus' little plot of land is symbolically placed: on one side (*hinc*) Hyblaean bees in the willow flowers whisper him to dreams; on the other (*hinc*) the pruner sings to the accompaniment of doves, and the voice of the turtle is heard in the elm. So Virgil's art borders on Theocritus (Hybla is on the slopes of Mt. Etna) and on the verses of his friend Gallus (Otto Skutsch sees the reference to doves as an indirect quotation from one of Gallus' love elegies). See the discussion by William Berg in *Early Virgil* [London, 1974], pp. 153–4. In lines 38–9 of the same poem, the pines, fountains and woodlands that call Tityrus from Rome may be Virgil's themes calling to their poet. So Marie Desport, *L'Incantation Virgilienne* (Bordeaux, 1952), p. 119.

V Figures in a Landscape

1. A Chromis is mentioned in Theocritus 1.24 as a contestant in song from Libya (hence perhaps the hue in his name). Perhaps then Virgil's Chromis can provide the "shadow" for a Jungian hero myth in *Eclogue* 6. See fn. 8 in Chapter XIII.

2. So Northrup Frye, *Milton's Lycidas* (New York, 1961), pp. 200–1.

3. In keeping the figures bearing the same name one character throughout the *Eclogues*, I follow the lead provided by John Van Sickle in *The Design of Virgil's Bucolics* (Rome, 1978) and T. E. S. Flintoff, "Characterization in Virgil's *Eclogues*" *PVS* 15 (1975–6), pp. 16–26.

There are serious problems with this approach, however, and the stern comment of the greatest authority on Theocritus must be set forth here: "Nowhere is it plain that [in Theocritus] the same person is meant, and in some cases it is clearly not so." (A. S. F. Gow, *Theocritus* [Cambridge, 1950] vol. 2, p. 131, fn. 1) The two most difficult problems concern Daphnis in poems 5 and 7 and Damoetas in poems 2 and 3: each in the first of the poems in sequence is said to have died, and each is very much alive in the poems following. I take Daphnis' reappearance in 7 to be his epiphany as a god (see fn. 4 below), and Damoetas' "death" in 2 as mere love-sickness: the *moriens* given him in line 38 need no more imply he has died than does the *mori* given the speaker of the poem, Corydon, in line 7. Van Sickle's sensible approach, reading the poems in sequence, is to see the characters not as persons so much as thematic ideas accumulating significance with each reappearance—and that, in the end, is also my purpose in this book.

4. This is the most logical solution to the problem of Daphnis dying in *Eclogue* 5 and re-appearing in *Eclogue* 7, and the necessary consequence of insisting that the eclogues be read sequentially with the characters preserving one identity from poem to poem. Daphnis as *praesens divus* in *Eclogue* 7 is the daring suggestion first made, with some support from Servius, by William Berg in *Early Virgil* (London, 1974), pp. 130–1.

5. Interest in attempting to identify the characters as historical personages has waned in recent decades. For attempts to do so earlier in the century, see the ambitious Léon Herrmann, *Les Masques et les Visages dans les Bucoliques de Virgile* (Brussels, 1930) and the more sober Tenney Frank, *Vergil* (New York, 1922), pp. 110–21.

6. Eduard Norden's *Die Geburt eines Kindes* (Leipzig, 1924) gave the near-Eastern interpretation of the eclogue new respectability in our century: both Virgil's Sibylline source and various near-Eastern books including even the New Testament have drawn "messianic" details from the worship of the Greek-Egyptian principle Aion, a child-figure who symbolized rebirth in nature. Early Christian writers were suddenly closer to the truth about *Eclogue* 4 than were twentieth-century classicists. Norden's theory was eventually challenged by the almost equally controversial Günther Jachmann in "Die vierte Ekloge Vergils" *Annali della scuola normale di Pisa* 21 (1952), pp. 13–62. For a good discussion see Berg, *Early Virgil*, pp. 155–8.

7. Presumably Virgil didn't name the child either as Antony's or Octavian's for fear of offending one of the two most powerful men in the

world. He also saved himself thereby from embarrassment in case the expected *puer* of either world leader turned out to be a *puella*. As it happened, both Octavian and Antony were presented with daughters, Octavian's destined to be the notoriously profligate Julia—which apparently did not harm the reputation either of the *Eclogue* or of its author in later years. Pollio fathered two sons about the time of his consulship, one of whom, C. Asinius Gallus, afterwards claimed (see Servius Danielis on 4.11 [*inibit*]) to be the *puer*. Doubtless there were as many claimants to the honor as there are elderly Polish gentlemen today who claim to be the original of Thomas Mann's Tadzio. In an article as voluminous and impressive as his name, Ian M. LeM. Du Quesnay ("Vergil's Fourth *Eclogue*" *Papers of the Liverpool Latin Seminar* [1976], ed. Francis Cairns, pp. 25–99) argues that the *puer* is the one Antony awaited.

8. I owe a debt here to Robert Coleman, "Vergil's Pastoral Modes" in *Ancient Pastoral,* ed. A. J. Boyle (Melbourne, 1975), pp. 60–1. My grouping of characters differs, however, from his.

9. Eleanor W. Leach, *Vergil's Eclogues: Landscapes of Experience* (Cornell, 1974), p. 246.

VI   Music

1. It may be argued that the boy who surrenders subtly wins in Horace *Odes* 3.9, and that Énée similarly wins his Didon by losing to her in the Act IV amoebean love duet in Berlioz' *Les Troyens*. My own favorite amoebean exchange is Catullus 45, where the poet stands outside the dialogue commenting, and implying with subtle irony that, so long as love lasts, the lovers' verbal exchanges will never end; at the end of the poem there is as yet no clear winner in the contest.

2. In Virgil's day unsympathetic critics were quick to ridicule this. The *Vita Donatiana* records that Virgil's *quoium pecus* at the beginning of *Eclogue* 3 (a possible rendering might be "Tell me, Damoetas, *whoise flock* is that?") was parodied in the *Antibucolica* of a certain Numitorius as "Tell me, Damoetas, *whoise flock*—is that Latin?" and given the response, "No—that's just the way they talk in the country." It was a fairly devastating criticism of what may, after all, have been Virgil's first published line, and it may have deterred him from further attempts at realistic language.

3. Thomas G. Rosenmeyer, *The Green Cabinet: Theocritus and the*

European Pastoral Lyric (Berkeley, 1969), p. 148. The title of this perceptive and persuasive book comes from Spenser's "December" and is one more designation for what commentators have called pastoral's enclosure, *locus amoenus,* or pleasance.

4. See *The Eclogues of Virgil,* tr., intro. (Melbourne, 1976), p. 24. In his introduction Boyle provides perhaps the only overall view of the *Eclogues* that touches on all important points and derives from them a consistent point of view. I have reworked his "constituents" here to some degree, mainly to fit them into the order in which Virgil takes them up, but I intend thereby no criticism of Professor Boyle's important work.

5. See *inter alia Georgics* 1.496; 2.285; 4.345, 375, 400, *Aeneid* 1.464; 3.304; 4.449; 5.673; 6.269, 505, 885; 7.593; 10.465, 758; 11.49; 12.906.

6. See "The Two Voices of Virgil's *Aeneid*" in *Virgil: A Collection of Critical Essays,* ed. Steele Commager (Englewood Cliffs, 1966), pp. 122–3. See also M. Owen Lee, *Fathers and Sons in Virgil's Aeneid* (Albany, 1979), pp. 165–6.

7. The first events (lines 41–42) seem to be wrenched violently out of sequence: Virgil lists the repeopling of the earth after the flood, then the reign of Saturn in Italy, then the punishment of Prometheus, and finally Prometheus' theft of fire. The apparent difficulty in this disappears if we allow our poet an excited four-term *hysteron proteron.* Further, Atalanta seems not to fit with the other unfortunates. But Virgil may have in mind Venus' metamorphosis of Atalanta and Hippomenes into lions as punishment for their coupling in Cybele's temple or, as the *mala* of *Eclogue* 8 bring a *malus error* to the innocent boy there, the fault of Atalanta *miratam mala* may be preoccupation with erotic desires. (Cf. Theocritus 3.41–2: "Atalanta saw the apples, and madly longed for them, and fell into the deep waters of desire.") In any case, the difficulties here ultimately stem from our loss of Gallus' poetry and that of the Alexandrian predecessors, especially Callimachus and Euphorion, he would have used.

8. While it may be true to say, with Renato Poggioli in *The Oaten Flute* (Harvard, 1975), p. 8, that the Arcadian shepherd "is obsessed by neither temptation nor guilt, and is free from the sense of sin" (i.e., personal sin, especially "in the realm of sex"), it should also be remarked that no figure that speaks in Virgil's Arcadia is without some inkling that there is a flaw in human nature which makes the attainment of perfect bliss impossible. Mythologies have thought this awareness of human

fallibility the result of man's evolving into his conscious state (the "sins" of Prometheus, Pandora, Psyche, and Eve are all sins of coming to know), and have attached a sense of guilt to it. I regret that I have no more precise term to use for this than the "original sin" of Christian theologies, as the idea is important for any understanding of the songs of Silenus and Damon, and of Virgil's work as a whole.

9. Other candidates are the third-century Archimedes, an associate of Conon, or the earlier Eudoxus whose writings, *via* Aratus, provided Virgil with much astronomical detail for the *Georgics*.

10. Servius Danielis on 3.105 records that Asconius Pedianus heard Virgil say that he made the riddles "a trap for scholars" (*grammaticis crucem*); that the answer to the first was "the tomb of Caelius" (the Latin *Caeli* could mean either "of the sky" or "of Caelius," and Caelius was a Mantuan who wasted his inheritance and was left with only three ell's space for burial). Virgil was very likely twitting the inquiring scholar.

11. Palaemon may not be just the neighbor the boys say he is. He could, in Virgil's Arcadia where both fresh and salt water gods come and go, be the sea god Palaemon, and so expected to use the watery response he does to end the contestants' poetic outpourings: "Close the flood-gates, boys. The meadows have had enough to drink."

12. That *Eclogue* 7 is an *ars poetica* is argued, with his characteristically humane approach, by Viktor Pöschl in *Die Hirtendichtung Virgils* (Heidelberg, 1964), pp. 150 ff. A less solemn appreciation is Charles Fantazzi and Carl W. Querbach, "Sound and Substance: A Reading of Virgil's Seventh Eclogue" *Phoenix* 39 (1985), pp. 355–67.

VII Love

1. Charles Fantazzi, "Virgilian Pastoral and Roman Love Poetry" *AJP* 87 (1966), p. 171.

2. The opening lines may come from Phanocles' *Erotes,* and many of the details from Meleager's *Garland*. See William Berg, *Early Virgil,* pp. 113–4.

3. Catullus wrote a cycle of poems to the boy Juventius, but scholarly opinion favors the view that these were not written out of an actual affair but as a kind of trap set for his critics. They could also have been written out of a need for some Horatian distancing.

4. See M. Owen Lee, "Catullus in the Odes of Horace" *Ramus* 4 (1975), pp. 33–48.

5. Ronald Syme, in Chapter II ("The Hazards of Life") of *The Augustan Aristocracy* (Oxford, 1986), pp. 22–3, suggests that a plague may have carried off Catullus along with Calvus, Lucretius, and other public figures "not heard of subsequent to 54". Similarly many of the young artists of the nineteenth century were claimed by syphilis. The fact remains that an overwhelming percentage of lyric artists die, from whatever causes, in their thirties or earlier.

6. The two authors are quoted from Peter V. Marinelli, *Pastoral*, pp. 79–80.

7. Eleanor M. Leach, *Vergil's Eclogues: Landscapes of Experience*, p. 154.

8. Charles Fantazzi, *AJP* 87 (1966), p. 181.

9. See G. W. Bowersock, "A Date in the *Eighth Eclogue*" *HSCP* 75 (1971), pp. 73–80, and John Van Sickle, "*Commentaria in Maronem Commenticia:* A Case History of *Bucolics* Misread," *Arethusa* 14 (1981), pp. 17–34.

10. Peter V. Marinelli, *Pastoral*, p. 72.

11. *The Eclogues of Virgil*, tr. intro., p. 21.

VIII   The City

1. See M. C. J. Putnam, "Virgil's First Eclogue: Poetics of Enclosure" *Essays on Latin Lyric, Elegy, and Epic* (Princeton, 1982), esp. pp. 262–3.

2. *European Literature in the Latin Middle Ages*, tr. W. R. Trask, p. 190.

3. See especially Adam Parry, "The Two Voices of Virgil's Aeneid" in *Virgil: A Collection of Critical Essays*, ed. Steele Commager, pp. 107–23.

4. See Servius on *Aeneid* 10.198–200. For different interpretations see William Berg, *Early Virgil*, pp. 141–2.

IX   The Golden Age

1. Horace and Virgil probably did not become friends till two years after the date usually assigned *Eclogue* 4, in 38 B.C. when Virgil left the patronage of Pollio (in Antony's following) for that of Maecenas (in Octavian's). It seems best to say, with Du Quesnay (*Papers of the Liverpool Latin Seminar,* 1976, p. 76), that *Eclogue* 4 was written first, in the excitement following the Peace of Brundisium, and *Epode* 16 followed when it became clear that hostilities were breaking out again.

2. See Boyle's notes on lines 4, 6, 10, 13, 15f., 26f., 31–6, 40, 46, and 63 in *The Eclogues of Virgil* (Melbourne, 1976).

3. Du Quesnay (*Papers of the Liverpool Latin Seminar,* 1976, pp. 78–9) quotes two passages Virgil may well have read.

4. Charles Fantazzi, "Golden Age in Arcadia" *Latomus* 33 (1974), p. 304.

5. So John Van Sickle, *The Design of Virgil's Bucolics* (Rome, 1978), p. 239.

6. See William Berg, citing Léon Herrmann, in *Early Virgil,* p. 165.

7. Charles Fantazzi, *Latomus* 33 (1974), p. 304.

8. Antony made much of his descent from Hercules, "in his propaganda, on his coins, and in his style of dress" (Du Quesnay, *Papers of the Liverpool Latin Seminar,* 1976, p. 37). Octavian's claim to divine ancestry through Aeneas and Anchises became, of course, the subject of Virgil's *Aeneid.*

9. See *Early Virgil,* pp. 158–77.

X   Death

1. Erwin Panofsky, to whom this and all discussions of the famous phrase are indebted, traces the *memento mori* tradition from Poussin (in the Devonshire collection) through Reynolds and Cipriani to Evelyn Waugh in *Brideshead Revisited,* and the incorrect "nostalgic" tradition from Poussin (in the Louvre) through Diderot, Goethe, and Schiller. See "Et in Arcadia Ego," *Philosophy and History: Essays Presented to Ernst Cassirer* (Oxford, 1936), pp. 223–254.

2. Cf. Otto Skutsch, "Symmetry and Sense in the *Eclogues*" *HSCP* 73 (1969), p. 166: *Eclogue* 5 is "numerically exactly in the center of the

structure: it is preceded by 330 lines, the total of *Eclogues* i–iv, and followed by 331, the total of *Eclogues* vi–ix." John Van Sickle notes further refinements in *The Design of Virgil's Bucolics* (Rome, 1978), p. 23.

3. Virgil's "Death of Daphnis" also draws, with considerable differences, from the post-Theocritean *Lament for Adonis* by Bion and the anonymous *Lament for Bion*.

4. William Berg, *Early Virgil,* pp. 15–22, also finds connections with Apollo, Dionysus, Orpheus, Prometheus, Paris, Anchises, Enkidu, and David.

5. See Eleanor M. Leach, *Vergil's Eclogues: Landscapes of Experience,* p. 188.

6. See, for example, Guy Lee, "A reading of Vergil's fifth Eclogue" *Proceedings of the Cambridge Philological Society* 203 (1977), esp. pp. 67–9. And though we never feel that there are two different aspects of Milton's personality at work in *Lycidas,* Renato Poggioli, in *The Oaten Flute* (Harvard, 1975), p. 76, notes that the poet "plays at once the roles of Mopsus and Menalcas, first weeping over the death of his Lycidas and then rejoicing at his ascent among the blessed."

7. With Tristan and Isolde there is, of course, the important difference that they die of unfulfilled but not, as with Daphnis, unrequited love.

XI Leaving Arcadia

1. See Servius on 10.46 *(nec sit mihi credere tantum): hi autem omnes versus Galli sunt, de ipsius translati carminibus.* It need hardly be said that much that is obscure in the *Eclogues* would be clear if we had more of the writings of Virgil's predecessors and contemporaries.

XII Reading the *Eclogues*

1. For a good analysis of the problem along these lines, see Robert Coleman, ed. *Vergil: Eclogues* (Cambridge, 1977), pp. 14–21. (My own order differs somewhat from his.) It is of course always possible that the prefatory remarks addressed to politically involved figures, from which some of the poems are dated, were added after the composition of the poems proper. For twenty different opinions on the matter of order of

composition, see Edward Coleiro, *An Introduction to Vergil's Bucolics* (Amsterdam, 1979), p. 93.

2. Edward Coleiro (above, note 1), pp. 283–4, dates *Eclogue* 10 to the year 37 B.C.

3. Guy Lee, in his skillful verse-for-verse translation *Virgil, The Eclogues* (Harmondsworth, 1984), p. 14, fn. 4, suggests that the term "came from the grammarians' habit of referring to Piece 1, Piece 2, etc.," somewhat along the line, I might add, of musical opus numbers. Lee says further that the French *Eglogue* and the Italian *Egloga* are derived from "the bogus etymology *Aig-loga*, 'Goat-talk'."

4. *Bucolica scripsit. Sed non eodem ordine edidit, quo scripsit. Appendix Serviana* in *Servii Grammatici*, ed. Georg Thilo and Hermann Hagen (1881–7, repr. Hildesheim, 1961), vol. 3, fasc. 2, p. 328.

5. See Ovid, *Amores* 1.15.25; Calpurnius 4.62–3; Virgil, *Georgics* 4.566.

6. *Eclogue* 8, with its two contrasting but self-contained songs, is not a dialogue, as Virgil makes clear by shifting gears between the two halves at lines 62–3: *vos, quae responderit Alphesiboeus, / dicite, Pierides: non omnia possumus omnes.*

7. See "Le Secret de Virgile et l'Architecture des Bucoliques," *Lettres d'Humanité* 3 (1944), pp. 71–147. Maury himself acknowledged a debt to E. Krause, *Quibus temporibus quoque ordine Vergilius eclogas suas scripsit* (Berlin, 1884).

8. Maury's thesis was accepted enthusiastically by his compatriot Jacques Perret (*Virgile: L'Homme et L'Oeuvre* [Paris, 1952], pp. 14–8) and eventually in outline by the Americans George Duckworth "The Architecture of the *Aeneid*" AJP 75[1954], p. 4), Brooks Otis (*Virgil: A Study in Civilized Poetry* [Oxford, 1964]. p. 129), and John Van Sickle, *The Design of Virgil's Bucolics* [Rome, 1978], pp. 20–1, 27–8). For a cooly reasoned assessment of Maury's and other attempts to explain the arrangement of the *Eclogues,* see the chapter "Architecture" in Niall Rudd, *Lines of Enquiry* (Cambridge, 1976).

9. See "Symmetry and Sense in the Eclogues" *HSCP* 73 (1969), pp. 153–69. Skutsch had little sympathy with Maury when he first touched on the subject, in "Zu Vergils Eklogen" *Rh.M.* 99(1956), pp. 193–201.

10. See "The Original Form of the Second Eclogue" *HSCP* 74 (1970), pp. 95–9.

11. See George E. Duckworth, *Structural Patterns and Proportions in Vergil's Aeneid* (Ann Arbor, 1962).

12. *Early Virgil*, pp. 110–1.

13. "The Book-Roll and Some Conventions of the Poetic Book" *Arethusa* 13 (1980), p. 5.

14. Ibid., p. 16.

15. See M. Owen Lee, "Virgil as Orpheus" *Orpheus* 11 (1964), pp. 9–18.

16. Scholarly opinion is still divided on the matter of whether lines 1–40, addressed to Allius, are a part of 68 or a separate poem. A good argument for the lines belonging, indeed being essential, to poem 68 and having an influence on the young Virgil may be found in Gordon Williams, *Tradition and Originality in Roman Poetry* (Oxford, 1968), pp. 229–39.

17. *The Idea of Lyric* (Berkeley, 1982), p. 159.

XIII   Interpreting the *Eclogues*

1. See C. G. Jung, *Four Archetypes*, tr. R. F. C. Hull (London, 1972), p. 50. The paper was first published as "Die verschiedene Aspekte der Wiedergeburt" *Eranos Jahrbuch 1939* (Zürich, 1940).

2. For a Christian comment on the correspondences between the mythic archetypes and the historical Jesus, see Victor White, *God and the Unconscious* (London, 1952), especially Chapter XII, "The Dying God".

3. *Four Archtypes* (above, note 1), pp. 65–6.

4. Peter V. Marinelli, *Pastoral*, p. 38.

5. See "The Psychology of the Child Archetype," tr. R. F. C. Hull, reprinted in *Psyche and Symbol* (New York, 1958), pp. 113–31.

6. This is my interpretation, in *Fathers and Sons in Virgil's Aeneid* (Albany, 1979), pp. 101–4, 142–3, and 155–6.

7. This translation is based on an interpretation offered by Rory B. Egan, "*Satis est potuisse videri,*" *CW* 73 (1980), pp. 379–83, in which parallels are drawn from the capture of the Jewish Asmodeus and the Irish leprechaun.

8. Archetypally, the hero befriends what Jung calls his shadow

before encountering his *anima*-figure and his wise old man. Could Virgil have intuited this when he called his two young heroes Mnasyllus ("remembering the forest," i.e., exploring his unconscious past) and Chromis ("color," i.e., the shadow)?

9. See Charles Segal, "Two Fauns and a Naiad?" *AJP* 92 (1971), pp. 56–61.

10. Compare the red berry juice smeared on Pan *quem vidimus ipsi* in *Eclogue* 10.26–7, and the further details from other mythologies offered in Egan (above, note 7), fn. 12.

11. Eleanor M. Leach, *Vergil's Eclogues: Landscapes of Experience,* p. 234, fn. 1, adroitly compares Silenus' "for the lass here a different answer" with Socrates' *alla toutōn men eisauthis se timōrēsomai* (*Symposium* 213d).

Index of Names

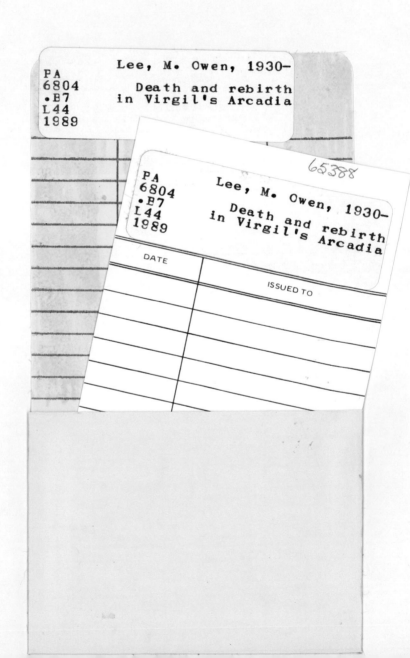